# NORTHAMPTONSHIRE
# RAMBLES

Stan and Jean

Christmas 1992

*Countryside Books' walking guides cover most areas of England and Wales and include the following series:*

County Rambles
Walks for Motorists
Exploring Long Distance Paths
Literary Walks
Pub Walks

*A complete list is available from the publishers:*

3 Catherine Road, Newbury, Berkshire

# NORTHAMPTONSHIRE RAMBLES

## Fourteen Country Walks around Northamptonshire

### Mia Butler

———

### With Historical Notes

**COUNTRYSIDE BOOKS**
NEWBURY, BERKSHIRE

First Published Mia Butler 1991
© Mia Butler 1991

Revised and Reprinted 1992

COUNTRYSIDE BOOKS
3 Catherine Road
Newbury, Berkshire

ISBN 1 85306 119 0

Cover photograph of Newnham Village
taken by Norma Pearson

Produced through MRM Associates Ltd., Reading
Typeset by Plexus Design Consultants, Aldershot
Printed in England by J. W. Arrowsmith Ltd., Bristol

For Bug, my nearest and dearest, with love.

# Contents

Sketch map showing locations of the walks.

# Introduction

Northamptonshire has been dubbed the 'County of squires and spires' and that is very close to the truth! Nestled almost in the heart of England, there are many fine country houses, wealthy estates, manors and mansions. There are magnificent stone churches and castles to delight those who take the time to stop and stare, conservation villages, ancient monuments, follies and museums, all contributing to the heritage of our county.

The oldest rocks are in the west, being about 190 million years old, and these Jurassic beds gently tilt to the south-east. Quarrying has left a multitude of scars in the region, but by default has enabled archaeologists to expose priceless artefacts and hopefully, when such sites are finally restored, will provide other benefits. Present day gravel extractions reveal beds of clay, where it might be thrilling to discover an ammonite or even fossil remains of a dinosaur!

Through the middle of the county winds the river Nene, a vital trade highway in the dim distant past, accounting for the settlements of Iron Age man, the Romans, and countless others over the succeeding centuries.

The remnants of the once vast Royal hunting forests of Rockingham, Salcey and Whittlebury were favoured by Kings, right back to Norman times, when the death penalty was imposed for the stealing of deer. And was not Whittlebury deemed to be the final resting place of Boadicea? Charles I felled much of the forest in order to build ships for his navy, and further serious depletion of ancient woodland was caused by some Victorian landowners, when cereals engendered a higher financial return and tree stocks were decimated in certain areas.

Today busy market towns, sleepy villages and hamlets vie with sprawling urban development, but above all the countryside survives. There is an abundant variety of terrain, with ancient ridge and furrow meadows, spangled skeins of waterways and streams, and hills and valleys to waylay any monotony.

Country Parks, nature trails and reserves, S.S.S.I.'s (Sites of Special Scientific Interest) and 2,000 miles of public footpaths, allow access for all, to satisfy the needs of every rambler. Up hill or down dale, there is always something to intrigue, be it old village pumps or stocks on the green, in what I personally see as the subtle 'patchwork' of my county.

I hope that I have pointed the way to some of these. Hidden treasure awaits discovery by the curious walker and these 14 circular walks are an introduction to Northamptonshire's variety. The historical notes are designed to provide basic information about the places of interest along the route and will be found at the end of each chapter. For those who like to stop along the way, the names of good pubs and places serving refreshments along or near the route are mentioned.

Sketch maps accompany each walk but more detailed information can be gained from the relevant 1:50,000 Ordnance Survey map in the Landranger series. When appropriate, please remember the Country Code and make sure gates are not left open or any farm animals disturbed. No special equipment is needed to enjoy the countryside on foot but do wear a stout pair of shoes and remember that at least one muddy patch is likely even on a sunny day.

The preparation and fieldwork for this collection of walks has been a 'labour of love'. I sincerely hope that you will find pleasure in pursuing them, and so discover more of this captivating countryside.

Mia Butler
May 1992

# East Carlton, Middleton and Cottingham: The Vale of the Welland

**Introduction:** In the north of the county, not far from the border with Leicestershire, East Carlton Countryside Park covers 100 acres of the slopes overlooking the extensive Welland Valley, where the river of the same name flows in the hollow. The sweeping vistas here open to the village of Bringhurst, over the lush fields of the Welland Valley, and spinneys with such charming names as Back Hook and Shoulder of Mutton.

Viewed from the ridge above, the villages of Middleton and Cottingham have a mixture of old and new dwellings, resulting in a kaleidoscope of multi-hued rooftops set in a higgledy-piggledy fashion below. Just along the road (B670) from Cottingham (no direct footpath) is the dramatic Rockingham Castle, stronghold of Saxon warriors and fortress of William the Conqueror. Smooth, gentle hills, copses rising from grassy knolls, verdant pastures and hamlets merging into green landscapes stretching away to infinity, are generously spread throughout this invigorating walk.

**Distance:** Roughly 3½ miles. The shorter circuit about 1 mile less. There is one particularly steep hill to be negotiated. OS Landranger 1:50,000 Sheet 141.

**Refreshments:** In the park Centre, the cafeteria is open throughout the year. In Middleton, the Red Lion public house, and the Spread Eagle in Cottingham offer food and drink, as does the Hunting Lodge Hotel and Restaurant.

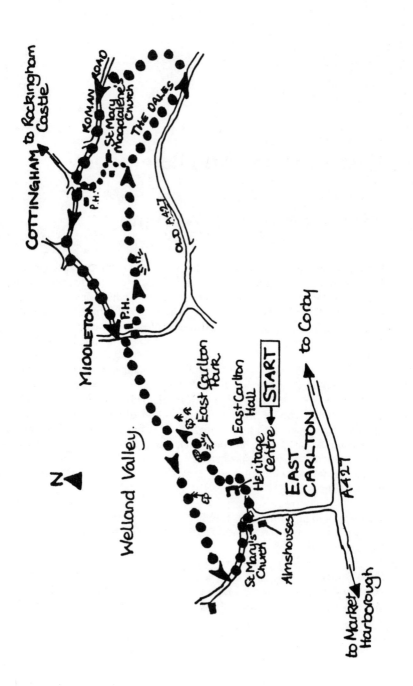

**How to get there:** East Carlton Countryside Park is located 4½ miles to the west of Corby, off the A427, toward Market Harborough. There is a limited bus service between these two towns. The walk begins at the Heritage Centre in the Park.

**The Walk:** Having paused for a moment to enjoy the sweeping views, begin the walk by leaving the Heritage Centre behind. Head down the path, which goes between the two natural ponds, serviced by a stream running down to the river Welland. Moorhens, mallards and other feathered visitors are often busy here. Go over the wooden bridge and under the mature beeches and chestnuts to join the level path which runs along the lower side of the boundary fence. Pass the curious 'squeeze' stile and kissing-gate, one of many yet to come.

Emerging at Middleton Hill, a pair of handsome stone cottages with mullioned windows stand opposite, dated on a tablet AD1862, adjacent to the Red Lion public house. On the near side of the hill is more natural stone in the long wall, and a horse trough built into it is inscribed 'IHP 1844' (referring to the prominent local Palmer family), fed by a lively spring of pure water.

Crossing the road, turn into School Hill, curving round the bend, which is *extremely* steep. Do pause at intervals and look over your shoulder at the unfolding panorama, before turning at the top into Camsdale Walk.

On this corner an old iron pump remains, with an acorn on the handle and sporting a fancy spout, leaving us a solid reminder of the villagers' chore of having to fetch their water. The Old School House occupies an enviable elevated position here, with enchanting views in every direction.

Continue along the crest of the hill between overgrown low stone walls, where half-hidden homes blend into the side of the scarp, and by the rear of the 17th century three-storeyed Bury House. Through the green iron kissing-gate, the rectory, weathervane and soaring spire of the church of St Mary Magdalene are now revealed. For the short cut, follow the path to the left, past the church and down the steps to Church Lane, to the centre of Cottingham.

On the right, The Dales is shaped like an elongated dish, rising to the east. Owned by the church since 1600, only cows were ever grazed there for centuries. This special corner has now changed hands and may now bask in the protection of being designated as a Pocket Park. This sheltered and compact little valley is also much appreciated as a splendid patch for tobogganing in the winter, and has an interesting cache of flora for the botanist in spring and summer.

A spring pops up briefly in the dip, before quickly being swallowed up again underground. Tall chestnut trees enhance this spot and in the far corner, beneath one of these, concrete steps lead to the lane (old A427). In about 20 yards on the left, a fingerpost and stile indicate the path, first by the hedge, and then over open fields, going toward the houses in the distance.

At the Roman Road, turn downhill at Millfield past the Methodist church and the bus shelter, bearing left to meet Church Lane (where the shorter walk exits), into High Street (and the B670 for Rockingham Castle), with the Spread Eagle pub on the corner.

Follow the long wall around The Hunting Lodge, past the War Memorial, to the stone parish boundary marker on the verge, at Middleton. Several older houses edge the street here, including The Old Forge, now restored, the old Congregational church, and a house with a lantern in the roof. There is a late 18th century Georgian house with a fine doorway, elegant gateways and conservatories. Previous excavations for new bungalows unearthed part of a Roman mosaic floor.

Round the corner, at the bottom of Middleton Hill, return to the fingerpost 'To East Carlton', retracing your steps to the initial path. Continue past the entire length of the park in a straight line to the hamlet of East Carlton, and watch out for the sign 'Trespassers will be shot'! Time to admire here the dressed stone walls and arched windows of the dignified church of St Peter, and the delightful almshouses. The angular spiked gates between stone columns at the entrance to the Park lead to the driveway flanked by crab apple and cherry trees, lending a cheery welcome to visitors in the springtime. This will bring you back to the Heritage Centre where you began your walk.

## Historical Notes

**East Carlton Park** was originally owned by the Palmer family, who built this grand Hall in 1873, in place of an earlier house dating back prior to 1723. The present Hall, with its somewhat austere symmetrical facade, is built of red brick and ironstone in the mode of a French chateau. It is now privately owned, and said to be haunted.

**East Carlton Countryside Park** is owned and managed by Corby District Council, the main building converted from an 18th century coach house and stables. The site warden will be pleased to assist with general information, and leaflets on walks are available. A 'smithy' complete with an anvil, forge and an array of blacksmiths' tools, nature trails, and what is claimed to be the largest lime tree in England, are just a few of the attractions in the beautiful parkland surrounding the Hall.

Part of the Industrial Heritage Centre, on the ground floor, is devoted to a permanent exhibition of the iron and steel industry, now in decline, for which nearby Corby was famous. It illustrates the history of the iron workings from Iron Age man onwards, and the progression from ore to steel. Workshops on the upper floor of the Centre disclose craft studios, most demonstrating arts such as glass blowing, wood turning, pottery and photography, run by traditional craftspeople, plus a gift shop.

Huge pieces of allied industrial equipment used in the steel workings are set about the spacious forecourt. There is a giant bucket from a dragline excavator which operated in the 1950s. This monster actually 'walked' along the quarry, as mining advanced, and is still remembered by the local wags when it first appeared on the scene. The cab was the size of a tennis court, and the bucket could carry an entire football team! There are also cast metal ingots and a slag pot for collecting this material in the mighty blast furnaces. The gargantuan structures of the plant have now virtually disappeared from the original site in Corby. These, and other relics, provide irresistible and provocative play places for children, who find all sorts of ways of enjoyment. A bright yellow train on display, which was also used in the works, makes an exciting object for clambering and climbing. On the cobbled forecourt, sturdy outdoor furnishings cater for those wishing to use the facilities of the cafeteria or simply to appreciate the wonderful scenery.

**Cottingham:** The church of St Mary Magdalene contains a large chest for important parish and ecclesiastical documents, and bears the date 1619. A feature of the decorated church capitals is the unique placing of four figures, two ladies with wimples and two knights, all in an horizontal position and thought to be from the 13th century, as is the south arcade and chancel. Richard Bancroft, an early rector, in 1586 became Chaplain to Sir Christopher Hatton, Queen Elizabeth I's Chancellor, and was eventually appointed Archbishop in 1604. He was responsible for the Authorised Version of the Bible.

At the foot of the steps, in Church Street, was a wash-pond for the cleaning of carts.

In Water Lane, the oldest surviving part of Cottingham, the houses were originally thatched, and the main road passed this way. There is a cruck-frame house (curved timbers supporting the roof), and Church House has mullioned windows. The Old Post Office, from the late 17th century, has an old fashioned bootscraper beside the door, and shows how the present level of the road surface has risen. Medieval pottery was found here at the depth of 1 metre.

Several strange stories exist in this area, having been handed down through generations, such as the sighting of a Roman centurion on the Roman Road. Another tale is of a black guardian dog, who appears from out of the dark and accompanies pedestrians over the hill, on the road to Rockingham, and apparently vanishes immediately if touched!

**East Carlton:** The impressive church of St Peter has beautiful clean-cut exterior lines, with graceful, arched windows, and was built in 1788, replacing a 14th century house of worship. The major monument is to Sir Geoffrey Palmer and his spouse, their upright, shrouded figures carved in alabaster and set in a shrine.

The superb row of almshouses, in yellow stone with moss bedecked slate, are set back from the lane facing the park. Inscribed over the centre 'Hospital of the Blessed Jesus in Carlton AD 1668', they were rebuilt in the Tudor style and 'more amply endowed' by their local benefactor Charlotte Palmer, in 1868.

# Pitsford, Holcot and Moulton

**Introduction:** Although this walk is the longest in this selection of rambles, it offers an assurance of serenity, created by this ponderous, tranquil spread of Pitsford Water, in the valley among the low lying hills. The panorama en route will enhance the walk as it unfolds, and there is a respite at the Holcot fishing lodge if desired.

Each village has dwellings of character and immense allure, set among comely gardens and consequently, is pleasing to the eye. A walk is permitted by Anglian Water around the western arm of the reservoir and gives access to Brixworth Country Park (NCC).

**Distance:** About 8 miles in all. OS Landranger 1:50,000 Sheet 152, Northampton and Milton Keynes. It should be noted that there are no short cuts or alternative rights of way, once the circuit is started.

**Refreshments:** All three villages have public houses and a few small shops.

**How to get there:** Pitsford Water is within easy reach of the county town, 5 miles to the north of Northampton, just off the Northampton-Market Harborough road (A508).

**The Walk:** Begin at Pitsford Water car park (pay and display), which is well signed from the main street of the village, and overlooks the dam and draw-off tower.

Leaving the car park, turn left downhill between high banks and trees meeting overhead, and over the causeway — a great haunt for

17

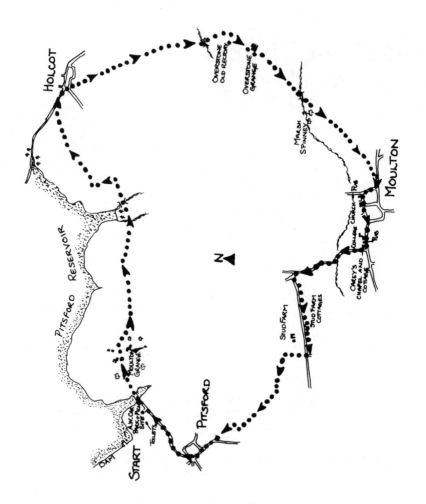

HOLCOT

OVERSTONE OLD RECTORY

OVERSTONE GRANGE

MARSH SPINNEY

MOULTON

PITSFORD RESERVOIR

OVERSTONE CHURCH RUIN

OVESLEY'S CHAPEL AND COTTAGES

STUD FARM

STUD FARM COTTAGES

N

MOULTON GRANGE

PITSFORD

BRIXWORTH PICNIC SITE

TOILETS

DAM

START

birdlovers. Carry on past the lodge on the private road (public footpath) to Moulton Grange, following the 'path' discs faithfully.

After the cattle grid, but before Grange Cottages, turn sharp right along the boundary fence of The Grange, to where the path continues along the south topside of the reservoir. There are fantastic views across to the spire atop the celebrated Saxon church tower at Brixworth, sweeping over to the distant causeway which bisects the water, below Holcot.

Zigzag through a tiny copse and forward, staying parallel with the water, on a good headland, to a second mixed broadleaf copse, over a stout plank and ditch, and over again to a similar clutch of trees, and stile in the corner. Go around the field edge, keeping the same general direction, into the dip and over the trickle, on the headland (not over the dyke in front) but round the corner for a few yards before crossing the ditch, bearing slightly left by the new pond. Carry on beside the trees and over the rise, with a glimpse of water between, to the lower corner.

Straight over the fine bridge, leaving the plantation behind, first on the perimeter, to a large disc and waymark, indicating a sharp left angle across the middle of the field toward a bungalow set close to the shoreline. Turn right at the stile to cross the access lane to North Fields and take a moment to pause here to appreciate the prospect. On again, beside an old cattle trough, toward Holcot, where the view now reveals the dam and car park on the far side of the open water. In the dip, go over the bridge, past the pond on the rise, taking an uphill diagonal track to the skyline and the Pitsford road, to enter the village. (Left for the fishing lodge for permits and leisure facilities.) Right now for Holcot crossroads, briefly on the Moulton road before crossing to the war memorial at the start of Back Lane.

A green fingerpost 'to Overstone' points to a large farm shed, so keep left around this to the next stile, which is clearly marked, over mixed farmland, now out of sight of the earlier route, past a pond with an island. At the far end of the third field, follow the hedgeline around two bends to a stile, where the bushes end abruptly. Go down this field and over the brook to divert to the right to a narrow stile in the fence. (Keep away from the main road as the path does not cross at any point.)

19

Follow the waymarks over the stone bridge and drive to The Old Rectory, to bear slightly left to two tall pine trees. Go through the farmyard past three black barns belonging to Overstone Grange and on through the paddock, now facing Moulton in the distance.

Keep to the stockproof fencing and over the little brick bridge, veering away from Marsh Spinney. Next traverse a huge undulating L-shaped field and at the corner of the industrial premises, slope off as directed, to the rim of houses and through the jetty to emerge opposite Prince of Wales Row.

Turn right into the old part of the village, past Dairy Farmhouse, going down Chater Street, past Rooty Hill cottage (hotel), following the beautiful dry stone wall into Church Street and The Artichoke pub.

At the ironstone parish church of St Peter and St Paul, on the mound, look up to see the sundial on the wall and the stone carvings of a pig and a sheep high on the roof.

Pass along steep Church Hill, lined with lovely stone homes, and the school, to West Street. Right now, through the village, past Moulton College, The Telegraph Inn adjoining Carey's Cottage and the chapel, before turning into Pitsford Road. A little road walking is required here, past Moulton Farm Nursery and Garden Centre. Just after this group of buildings, follow the fingerpost 'to Pitsford' toward a sparse line of conifers. Walk along the inside hedge, past Stud Farm Cottages, to where the trees peter out at Spectacle Lane.

Cross the Pitsford road and directly over next to Stud Farm, turning along the topside of the field and very briefly round the edge, then through the hedge, keeping next to it, toward Pitsford. In this field, follow around the curve and over an old stile, skirting a grand stable complex, and downhill on a fenced path next to paddocks to the lane and post 'to Moulton'.

Go down the street, bordered by the wall of Pitsford House, past elegant stone residences, The Chase, Manor Road and the school.

At the Green and phone box, a sign reads 'Pitsford Reservoir and Picnic Area', leaving the main street, into Grange Lane, bearing left under the big chestnut tree, to the Anglian Water signboards and car park.

## Historical Notes

**Pitsford Water:** Constructed in the 1950s for Anglian Water, Pitsford Water serves not only a functional purpose, but also as a refuge for wildlife, with a sizable sector set aside for nature conservation. It also features birdwatching, fly fishing for trout and horseriding (permits for all of these from the Holcot Fishing Lodge) and many other amenities.

Rare birds are known to have passed through or lingered here and have attracted a great deal of attention among 'twitchers' and novices alike. In autumn, it becomes a vital staging post for migrants, especially waders, and particularly in winter, many species of wildfowl are common in the area which is designated SSSI (Site of Special Scientific Interest).

The Sailing Club occupies a position on the far bank, and boats may be hired by the public from the fishing lodge.

**Moulton:** With much to offer in the way of interest, Moulton attracts further exploration at leisure.

Carey's Cottage, in West Street, close to the Baptist chapel, has a tablet on the wall, easily seen from the pavement. William Carey came from Paulerspury with his family, whence he was born in 1785, and pursued the trade of shoemaker. He became resident within the community as schoolmaster and pastor at the chapel, prior to taking up missionary work in India in 1793. His zeal in this calling led him into other worthy ventures, such as a translation of the Bible, the founding of a college of learning and the creation of a botanical garden, in addition to becoming a Professor of Languages. Some of his personal belongings are housed here for posterity.

The prestigious Moulton College of Agriculture, opened in 1921, embraces a cluster of working farms as well as tutorial and residential facilities, for a host of undergraduates. During World War II, from 1939-45, 1,300 women were recruited and trained here for the Women's Land Army, who were to replace farmworkers who had joined the forces. Courses were resumed as the men returned to 'civvy street' when more land and accommodation had to be found, as the Institute expanded and became recognised for its stalwart service to agriculture, attracting an increasing number of students to the establishment.

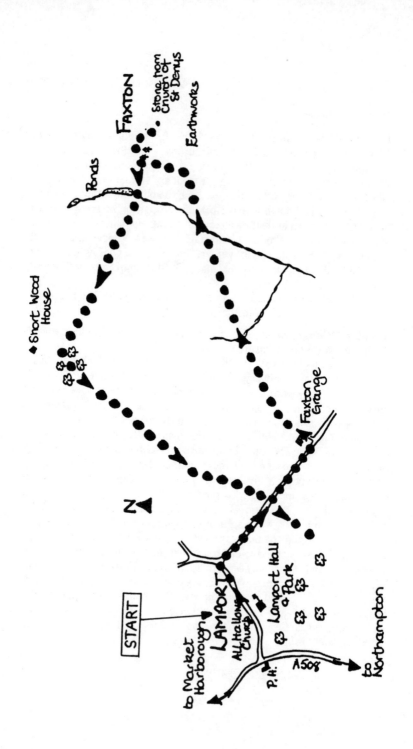

# Lamport and Faxton

**Introduction:** The small village of Lamport, once an estate community, consists of a single street of old stone houses and brick cottages, outside the boundary wall of historic Lamport Hall. The Hall, home of the Isham family for over 400 years, is now the venue for a wide range of cultural events, as well as outdoor shows and exhibitions.

Footpaths go off in several directions from here, but this particular route provides wide views over the beautiful surrounding countryside as well as a fascinating visit to the abandoned village of Faxton. Set on a hill, it is a choice vantage point. In the past the tiny hamlet, which stood in the middle of fields in total isolation, was sheltered by mighty elms and approached only through the meadows. Its decline began, some say, when the Plague was brought here from London by a servant. This exhilarating walk includes a range of woodland providing an ideal habitat for wildlife, and a glimpse of the unusual falconry tower of Short Wood House.

**Distance:** About 5 miles cross-country, taking 2½ hours at a leisurely pace. OS Landranger 1:50,000 Sheet 141.

**Refreshments:** The Swan pub is situated on the main road, not far from the main gates of the Hall. Amenities at Lamport Hall include teas, in summer, and a superb picnic area.

**How to get there:** Lamport is halfway between Northampton (8 miles) and Market Harborough.

**The Walk:** From the Hall, walk through the village and turn right at the T-junction of the B576 into the Old Walgrave road, and walk down as far as Faxton Grange.

The fingerpost points the way to the left, past the farm buildings, as the track curves past the front of a pair of cottages and through the gates to the grass fields. Go to the bottom of the hill and up and over the impending rise to the top, providing a good view of the rolling uplands.

Tall bushes and straggling trees mark the course of the brook, where the bridge in the corner may be hidden by heavy growth. Continue up the slope in the same direction in the first field, to a wooden bridge with side rails, on the incline, keeping in a straight line to merge with the broad track along the top of the hill. A little to the right, the earthworks of Faxton are barely discernible, adjacent to more recent plantations.

Stay on the bridleway, through the trees, and you may encounter the free-ranging, noisy peafowl — marvellous 'watchdogs' emitting shrill cries, running hither and thither about the spinneys! The lone private residence and breeding areas for game birds must be respected, as the walker goes slightly over the brow of the hill. Look to the right, to a rough 'island' in the midst of an arable field, to seek the one remaining stone from the church of St Denys, which marks the site of the deserted village of Faxton.

Return through the stands of conifers to enter a bridleway overlooking the attractive old fishponds, which are now a precious habitat for animals and birds. Down the hill and up yet again, with Short Wood House in the distance, which has a distinctive hawking (falconry) tower.

A gate opens to a young plantation, to the left, through which the path continues for a short way and then changes to follow the headland of the ensuing 3 fields, before spreading to the width of a bridleway.

Cross the road, next to a cottage on the corner and fingerpost to Hanging Houghton. The spinneys around the park are managed by the estate as a nature reserve and are a mix of broad-leaf trees, both native and more exotic varieties. Return through the tranquil enclosure to the point where the walk began.

**Historical Notes**

**Lamport:** Splendid gates by Hakewill, of 1824, greet the visitor at the main entrance to the spacious parkland of Lamport Hall. Mary Isham, lady of the house, planted a number of beautiful sycamore and cedar trees here in the 1820s, not far from the old cock-pit, a relic of the cruel sport of cockfighting.

Lamport Hall was the home of the notable Isham family from 1560, when it was purchased by John Isham for £510. It remained in their hands until Sir Gyles, 12th Baronet, and last of the line, died in 1976. They also owned another grand house at Pytchley, near to Kettering.

The first owner of the Hall, John Isham, built a new Elizabethan house 8 years later, which faced the church, and this building was subsequently modified by his grandson, Sir John. Later extensions and bays were designed in the period from 1654 to 1657 by John Webb, a protégé of the English architect, Inigo Jones. Stables were constructed in 1680, and further wings in 1732 and 1741, which added width to the front of the building. The establishment is now owned by the Lamport Hall Preservation Trust, and houses a superb library, distinguished furnishings and paintings.

The Rock Garden was very unusual at its inception. Situated at the side of the house, it was designed and implemented by Sir Charles, 10th Bart., who was an innovative and creative gardener. The dark rocks, towering to about 20 ft, became the backdrop for a group of gnomes brought over from Germany, which were set among the twisted paths and grottos.

**All Hallows' church**, opposite the Hall, houses the Isham Chapel, exclusive to members of that family. Built by Sir Justinian, 2nd Bart., with a vault beneath, it was finished in 1673. Records show that £80 was paid to Frank Smith, an 18th century master builder, for the monument to Sir Justinian, 4th Bart. Smith was also responsible for the Library wing at the Hall and the Rectory. The latter, built between 1727 and 1730, is next to the church and has panelled rooms, the original fireplaces of red Derbyshire marble and a very fine staircase.

Elizabeth, Lady Isham, wife of the same Baronet, died at the age of 47 years in 1713. She bore 14 children, 8 sons and 6 daughters. She merits a lengthy memorial inscription, which describes her great compassion. Floor slabs in the chapel include memorials to the Rev Euseby and Sir Edmund, as well as brasses to other members of the household.

Above the chancel arch in the main body of the church, is the Royal Arms of George II, and an iron screen divides the chapel and the chancel. The dark stained glass at first gives the impression of a painting in heavy colours. A processional cross of outstanding design, dated 1475, graces this house of worship.

**Faxton:** In Saxon times this was royal land and a village was recorded here in the 11th century. As the years progressed there was a manor house, almshouses and a brickworks, and fishponds to the north of the site are still in evidence. The last Squire of Faxton was John Nichols, who died mysteriously in the Lake District in 1616. He was a judge on circuit, presiding over a murder trial. It is said that he was poisoned by relatives of the accused, who evidently thought that by their action the miscreant could be saved from the ultimate punishment!

The army of Charles I rendezvoused here in June 1645 to rally for the Battle of Naseby against the Parliamentarians, who were led by their Commander-in-Chief, Sir Thomas Fairfax, and Oliver Cromwell, then Lieutenant-General of the Horse.

The precise cause of the decline and desertion of Faxton is unknown, although there has been much speculation. It is thought that the lord of the manor had fled from London at the onslaught of the Plague, but not before one of his servants had contracted the disease. If so, this could easily have spread rapidly through the isolated dwellers, as it did in other places. In the 18th century the Ishams of Lamport, who owned the estate at Faxton, razed the big mansion there, depleting the settlement even further.

The primitive church of St Denys, a simple edifice of Norman beginnings, was finally deconsecrated and demolished in 1958 and the 11th century font, plate and monuments distributed to Kettering, Lamport and the Victoria and Albert Museum in London, for safe keeping. A stone, encompassed by a fence, all sadly neglected, reads 'On this spot stood the altar of St Denys', and is the last reminder of the community which had survived here for centuries.

**Short Wood House** has a 3-storeyed tower, the oldest part, circa 1720, flanked by 2-storeyed wings. The upper window is thought to be fashioned from a chimneypiece brought over from Pytchley Hall. The falconry tower was used for the sport of hawking, and training the birds to attack their prey.

# Rothwell and Rushton

**Introduction:** Visitors to Rothwell, sometimes referred to locally as 'Rowell', will find much of interest, as this small place was once a prominent medieval town, built on a hill rising between the river Ise and Slade Brook. People flock here to the annual Rowell Fair; the traditional week-long street market charter was originally granted by King John in 1204, to Richard, Earl of Clare. The walk takes in the longest parish church in the county, the 16th century Jesus Hospital and Sir Thomas Tresham's Market House.

From Rothwell this fascinating walk bears out into the countryside, over the river Ise and across the fields, until the unparalleled Triangular Lodge comes into view. Also built by Sir Thomas Tresham in the late 16th century, it is an extraordinary monument based upon an interpretation of the Trinity. Rushton Hall also merits special attention, set in pleasant surroundings of mature woodland. Once upon a time, not so long ago, peacocks were frequently to be seen on the stone boundary wall of the parkland — alas, another scene gone forever!

**Distance:** About 5 miles, taking approximately 2½ hours, but allow time to relish the treasures. OS Landranger 1:50,000 Sheet 141.

**Refreshments:** There are several public houses in Rothwell, and the Thornhill Arms in Rushton.

**How to get there:** Rothwell is located 4 miles to the north-west of Kettering, on the A6 to Leicester road. Bus services operate on the main road, but are poor on weekends. Limited parking may be available at Squire's Hill, beneath the avenue of lime trees.

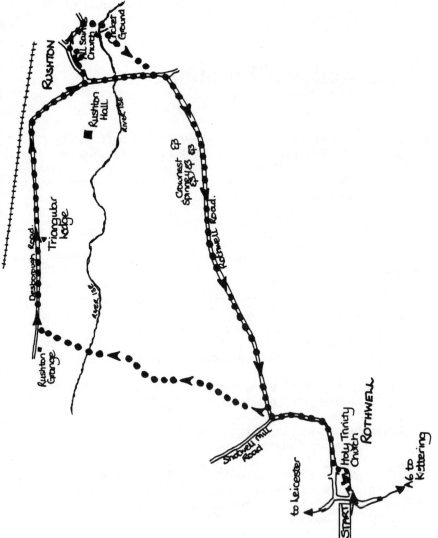

**The Walk:** The walk begins by the impressive bulk of Rothwell parish church of the Holy Trinity. Mellowed stone walls, traditional iron lamp-posts and a raised commemorative garden to one side, and Manor Park and what remains of a medieval fishpond on the other, provide a quiet background away from the bustle and din of the main through road.

The Georgian manor house enhances the approach to the massive church, where the path to the right is separated from the graveyard by tall black iron railings. This leads into Market Hill and the very old restored buildings of Jesus Hospital. Going up the Hill, Sir Thomas Tresham's Market House squats solidly beside the Old Red Lion public house, and the Church Sunday school. The whole of the town centre is now designated a conservation area.

Cross to the far side of the square, to a row of shops, walking to the right on the pavement. The Blue Bell Inn is facing, and the sign 'Bell Hill' is barely noticeable above a low doorway next to the street. The pedestrian walkway next to the pub leads into the Rushton Road. Follow this as far as Shotwell Mill Lane, and a few yards beyond the turn is the fingerpost 'Footpath'. Go through the iron gate, following the trodden path diagonally, negotiating a number of stiles with unusually high treads. Up the gentle hill and down again, with an occasional glimpse of Rushton Hall tucked away in the trees in the distance to the right.

Use the wooden bridge over the river Ise, sometimes no more than a trickle, and go up the track and over the stile in the split-log fence which encompasses 2 paddocks, close to Rushton Grange Farm.

Exit at the stile (almost lost in the hedgerow) signed 'Public footpath to Rothwell' on the Desborough to Rushton road. Bear to the right, where the remote Triangular Lodge is in sight. On reaching the long, winding stone wall, stop and take a look at this strange Lodge, before ambling on to the village. The railway line will be running parallel, and disappears under the bridge at the road junction to Pipewell.

Turning the corner toward Rushton, the walker may choose to take a slightly shorter route and carry on past Beech House driveway, by the fading glory of the gates of Rushton Hall, and over the hump-backed bridge.

Alternatively, turn into Station Road at the T-junction, and through the coffin-shaped graveyard surrounding the parish church of All Saints. The War Memorial overlooks the cricket ground, on the lower level, facing the Thornhill Arms, named after an early lord of the manor. In High Street, between the houses on the curve, the 'Footpath' sign directs the walker to further small paddocks in view of the far wall of the Manor House. Cross the wooden bridge and go straight forward to join the road near the bridge, following the winding wall of Rushton Hall grounds again.

Return via the Rothwell Road, with the Hall set snugly nearby amidst woodland comprising splendid chestnut, lime, silver birch, sycamore and other mature trees, and past the aptly named Crownest Spinney. The road will bring you back to Rothwell and the start of the walk.

## Historical Notes

**Rothwell:** Rothwell had a number of wells and springs acclaimed for their powers of healing, said to be due to the content of iron in the water. The Danish word 'Rodewell' meant 'the town with red water'.

Formerly known as St Saviour's, the parish church of the Holy Trinity has more than one claim to fame. It is the longest parish church in the county, measuring 173 ft, and signs indicate that it may have been even longer at one time. It also boasts the largest window. Oddly, the spire was never rebuilt after being struck by lightning, and demolished, in 1660. Within this noble interior, tombs and effigies of prominent families, notably the Treshams, repose in silent splendour.

The little doorway in the south porch leads down to the unique Bone Crypt, discovered accidentally by gravediggers in the 18th century, and one of only 2 left in England. Bones, that is human skulls, legs and thigh bones, are stacked here, but may eventually crumble to dust. They are thought to be the remains of bodies from the 13th century, when burial space seems to have been at a premium, variously thought to be as a result of a plague, or battle, or some unknown catastrophe.

**Jesus Hospital** was founded as almshouses by Owen Ragsdale in 1591. He had been a teacher at the Grammar School, and a former scholar of Magdalene College, Oxford, who later returned there to study Civil Law.

The male inmates of the hospital always wore blue coats right up to the 20th century. They received a small monetary allowance, medical help, and fruit from the garden. Peep through the gate to see the cobbled courtyard and the Principal's House, and the fields beyond, framed through the doorway.

**The Market House** on the spacious Market Square, was given to the town by Sir Thomas Tresham of Rushton. He was the lord of the manor of Rothwell. It is said that the mason was paid £62 for his labours, in about 1577, although the building remained unfinished for 300 years. The lord's estates were commandeered by the Crown after his implication in the Gunpowder Plot. The building had no roof and the arches were open for traders until J.A. Gotch designed and completed the roof in 1895. The round stairwell had been used as a jail! The frieze of heraldic shields around the hall, above the first floor, signifies the coats of arms of 90 landowners of the Rothwell Hundred (an historical administrative division of a county) and other families of importance.

**The Triangular Lodge** is an extraordinary edifice, classified as an Ancient Monument and administered by English Heritage (admission fee). It occupies a strategic corner in the grounds of Rushton Hall estate, and was also built by Sir Thomas Tresham, between 1594 and 1597. Entirely based on the Trinity, and constructed of light and dark banded limestone, each side measures 33 ft and 4 inches in length. It has 3 storeys, each with 3 windows on 3 sides, and lavish embellishments with trefoils (emblem of the Treshams), culminating in pinnacles. Sir Thomas had spent 13 years in prison for his religious beliefs before the building of this bizarre monument. Be it folly, flight of fancy or expression of faith, it is like no other and presents a bewitching puzzle to the beholder.

**Rushton Hall:** Sir Thomas made additions to Rushton Hall, an earlier Tudor house, fashioned from Weldon stone. His son, Francis inherited great wealth but was involved in the Gunpowder Plot and eventually died in the Tower of London in 1605, in the same year as his father. The Hall has now taken on a new role, as a special school for the blind.

**All Saints' Church**, built of ironstone, contains the marble effigy of William de Goldingham, a Knight Templar, who died in 1296. He is depicted with crossed legs, in fine chain armour complete with shield, buckle belt, sword and spur straps.

Sir Thomas Tresham, grandfather of the Sir Thomas previously mentioned, was the last English Lord Prior of the Knights Hospitallers (members of a religious and military Order originating at about the time of the first Crusade of 1096-99). The honour was bestowed upon him by Queen Mary, following her revival of the Order, and the dignified, bearded figure is shown wearing his robes of office, on an alabaster tomb-chest.

# Geddington and Newton:
# A Medieval Medley

**Introduction:** A walk for all seasons in an historic setting, the focal point is the picturesque conservation area at Geddington, where the elegant Eleanor Cross takes pride of place. A pleasant locale in which to linger, perhaps on the stone steps, within sight of the church of St Mary Magdalene, or on the ancient Old Bridge. Both villages boast delightful buildings of mellowed Weldon and Lincolnshire stone, with roofs of thatch or Collyweston slate. There are wide expanses of both pasture and woodland, where the more recent coniferous plantations blanket reclaimed ironstone quarries, in contrast to Geddington Chase, a remnant of the once vast Rockingham Forest which covered this land.

The route leads the walker along intriguing paths and opens to a compact valley of immense allure, passing a dovecote set above abandoned terraces and medieval fishponds, and views of surrounding forest landscapes. It is a walk eminently suitable for winter as well as summer, with the likelihood of spotting game and wild birds and an infinite variety of flora and fauna, particularly where the brook serves as a convenient 'corridor' for wildlife.

**Distance:** This is a leisurely saunter of about 3 miles, for those who like to 'stop and stare' (and smell the flowers!), with opportunities to meander along other footpaths within the boundaries of the parish of Geddington. OS Landranger 1:50,000 Sheet 141.

**Refreshments:** In Geddington, the Star Inn, the White Hart and the White Lion all offer hospitality in the way of food and drink. The Tea Shop, adjacent to the Eleanor Cross, is open at weekends.

WALK FIVE

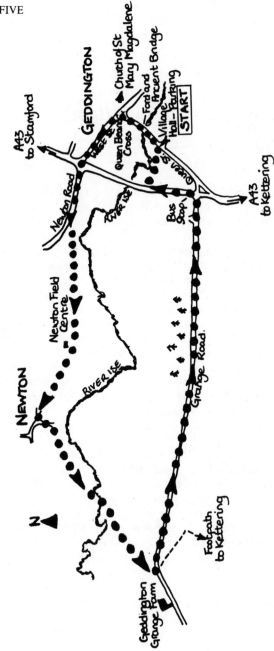

**How to get there:** Geddington is situated 4 miles north-east of Kettering on the A43 past Boughton House. Bus services operate from Kettering, Corby and further afield.

Approaching the village of Geddington, take the first turn on the right into Queen Street and look out for the sign 'Village Hall and Sports Complex', where there is ample car parking around the hall and spacious playing fields.

**The Walk:** The walk begins with a look around old Geddington. On the corner stands the old bakery, set back from the raised path (originally to prevent flooding) leading to the Old Bridge over the river Ise. Beside it, the ford is usually busy with a noisy gathering of ducks in the shallow water and on the silty islands overhung with weeping willows, creating an idyllic setting.

Standing where 3 roads meet, the Eleanor Cross invites attention. Also in the conservation area, designated in 1977, the Star Inn, the shop opposite which was the site of the original blacksmith's forge, and a huge granite boulder said to be a mounting block, outside The Tea Shop, all combine to form an attractive centre. The imposing church of St Mary Magdalene and the War Memorial complete the picture.

Follow West Street, to the left, where both stone and brick cottages line the pavements. The White Hart is located here, near to a quaint little jetty, one of several such nooks and crannies worthy of further exploration.

Just prior to the A43 crossroads, behind walls and lofty trees, lies the rambling vicarage, and there is an iron lamp-post on the path. Cross the busy highway with care, to Newton Road. At a green fingerpost 'Bridleway-Newton' on the left, go over the cattle-grid and through the farmyard to a grassy track, toward the medieval fishponds dominated by the fine Elizabethan dovecote.

In view is the Newton Field Centre, standing alone on the north side of the pretty Ise valley, with narrow gateways through which to squeeze into the graveyard, strewn with ancient headstones and embraced by ivy clad walls.

Forward now on a short stretch of access road to the village of Newton, once the scene of a bloody battle but now a serene hamlet of cottages and sturdy houses. Bear left at one of these, with dark moss on the grey slate roof and stone cattle troughs against the garden wall. Pass the phone box, to the bottom of the lane and over the stile (which may be obscured by the hedge at times), to a lower level over the undulating field.

Cross the wooden slatted bridge with handrails to a tranquil miniature meadow, with magnificent twisted and gnarled willow trees draped gracefully over the brook, making for a stile into woodland. The shady path winds its way beneath tall beeches, some with exposed root systems and trails of ivy clinging to the smooth trunks. Exit left on to Grange Road, a quiet back lane linking 2 main roads.

The vista here, locally known as Little Canada, overlooks the small valley, almost entirely hemmed in by woodland, and in the distance, Geddington Chase. On reaching the A43, turn left, walking a short way along the main road, where there are bus stops for both directions.

Just before the balustraded stone bridge over the Ise brook, go down the bank on the right-hand side of the road and take a field path through the meadow, with more handsome willows, iron lamp-posts and seats. A memorial plaque to Walter John, Duke of Buccleugh, 'who loved the countryside', stands in the grass, beside long-standing walls and a pool. This opens to a row of restored cottages, and emerges next to the Union Chapel and well-head, close to the village hall complex where you left your car.

## Historical Notes

**Geddington:** Numerous archaeological finds have demonstrated the existence of settlements in this area since Iron Age times. Flints and bones were discovered during ironstone quarrying in the 1970s, as well as Roman pottery and kiln materials, revealed in pits and ditches. In 1951, 10 iron-smelting furnaces and pottery of Roman origin came to light close to the Ise during pipelaying. Of later date, a medieval bronze badge depicting the Tudor Rose and a falcon, was found in the churchyard.

Formerly a Royal seat, in 1188 Henry II held a council here to raise money for an expedition to the Holy Land. In 1194, King Richard I of England played host to William, King of Scotland, and later, in 1201, King John granted and sealed the Borough Charter of Cambridge here.

**The Old Bridge**, spanning the river Ise since 1250, has a shallow ford beside it, and is a pleasant place to lean and take one's bearings. This narrow edifice carried all the traffic for many centuries. It incorporates 4 arches and 3 cutwaters, the latter's function being to resist the flow of water against the parapet, as well as offering safety and a passing place to travellers on the higher level.

**The Eleanor Cross:** Edward I, son of Henry III, with his adored wife Eleanor of Castile, were frequent visitors in their lifetime. After her death, in 1290, the funeral procession of Queen Eleanor halted at this spot on its way to Westminster from Harby in Nottinghamshire. Prior to this her husband is said to have laid her heart in Lincoln Cathedral. Four years later, the Cross was erected by the King, to mark the resting place of the cortege. Delicately carved by the artisans of the day, in Weldon stone, it also bears a darker band of the more robust and golden Stanion stone, just below the niche. Depicted on the face of the monument are roses, shields, and representations of the Queen, all topped by pinnacles. It is considered the best preserved of the 3 remaining Crosses on the 150 mile journey south. The penultimate stop to the final burial place was at Charing Cross in London.

The sunken well at the foot of the 7 steps has been in use since Roman times.

**The church of St Mary Magdalene** stands behind the Cross, creating a striking tableau amid the surrounding dwellings and school buildings. The church is similarly well preserved, containing a mix of styles. The tower has an octagonal spire and gargoyles, and inside, rounded 12th century arcades cut into Saxon walls. The chancel has a double clerestory on both sides, from the 13th and 15th centuries, and beautiful stained glass.

There are fascinating treasures to see, including the fine Jacobean carved oak screen, presented by the Tresham family, whose ancestors are remembered here. Many centuries ago there was a Royal palace close to the church, which was a popular resort of the Royal princes en route to the prolific hunting grounds of Rockingham Forest. Only pockets of the once extensive Forest have survived to this day, such as Geddington Chase, in close proximity to the village.

**The Vicarage**, built in 1851, was once, in part, a private preparatory school, where William Gladstone, the Liberal Prime Minister, and other prominent figures received their early education.

**Newton:** When the Tresham family became established here in the late 15th century they built Newton Hall, but it was demolished in the 18th century.

'Newtone' is mentioned in the Domesday survey, then later a record of 2 villages appears, 'Parva' and 'Magna', in 1262. In June 1607, the peace of the community was shattered when about a thousand armed peasants destroyed the hedges in protest at the enclosure of arable land for sheep pasture. Joshua Reynolds, nicknamed Captain Pouch because he carried a pouch of mysterious content, led the band, known as 'the Levellers'. They were suppressed by the local Justices of the Peace, condemned, hanged and quartered. The county later became renowned for the fine wool produced here.

**The Dovecote**, now scheduled as an Ancient Monument, stands squarely on a mound, dominating the group of medieval fishponds. An imposing gabled structure of stone, it was built by Maurice Tresham in the late 16th century, and is all that remains of the mansion's outbuildings belonging to this prominent family. The interior is divided into 2 parts, with 2 high windows and 2 low doors, and 2 raised outlets in the roof to accommodate 2,000 pairs of birds, with nesting boxes ranging the stout 3 ft thick walls. The inscription 'Tresham' may be seen high on the outer wall.

**Newton Field Centre** was once the private chapel of the Treshams, formerly St Faith's. The church itself ceased its religious role in 1959 and the memorials were removed to the church at Geddington, but the graveyard is still consecrated ground. The area provides a splendid habitat for many forms of wildlife, and consequently, for naturalist studies. Numerous courses in natural history are held in this unique setting, and it has proved to be of enormous interest and benefit to children and enthusiastic adults in extending their knowledge of the environment. .

The original church was a stone-walled barn-type building, with a steeply pitched roof and lime plastered inside. Later, in the 16th century, a short west tower was added, with a recessed broached spire and a single bell. In 1858 the main body of the church was rebuilt, the tower retained and 14th century windows set in place. A flagged floor was laid in the nave, and the whole finished with a slate roof.

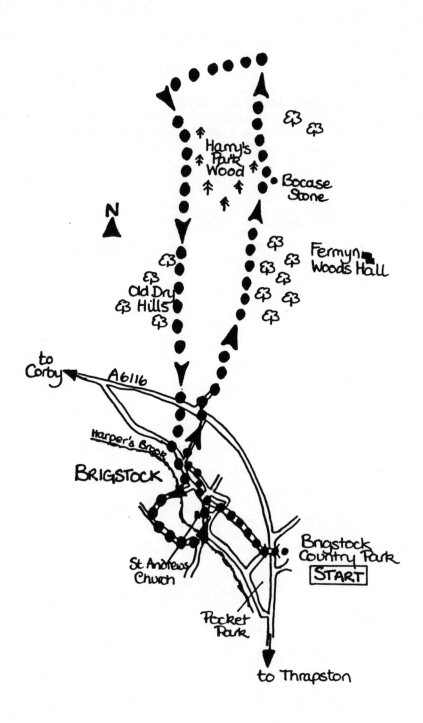

# Brigstock:
# The Bocase Stone

**Introduction:** A walk around the village of Brigstock and Harry's Park Wood is a step back into the past, with the added spice of perhaps spotting the elusive deer or other wildlife hidden within the cover of the woodland. In the Middle Ages this tidy village was one of the largest communities within the confines of the ancient Rockingham Forest, where the church bells tolled every day to guide travellers. It was owned by the Crown, and drastically deforested by Charles I, who needed the valuable timber from this and other forests to build ships for his Navy. It is now owned and managed by the Forestry Commission.

A surprise awaits the walker on the perimeter of Harry's Park Wood on this trail — the Bocase Stone, about which legends abound. Did Robin Hood really pass this way? The old buildings of Brigstock are of no lesser interest, and rightly include a conservation area in the hub of the village. A local character of the 19th century, the Rev. P.J. Sanderson, advised that his parish had 'the purest air in the world' and it is still a wonderful place for an invigorating walk.

**Distance:** Approximately 6 miles in all, which includes the village loop of about 1 mile. OS Landranger 1:50,000 Sheet 141.

**Refreshments:** The Olde Three Cocks and the Green Dragon public houses and shops.

**How to get there:** Brigstock is to the south-east of Corby on the A6116 bypass to Thrapston. Many amenities are available at Brigstock Country Park, formerly a sand-pit, and include plenty of car parking space and a Visitors Centre, although there are several other suitable places around the village if preferred. The walk begins from the Park.

**The Walk:** Leave the Park via the high footbridge over the bypass, descending by the steps beside the Pocket Park, to the Lyvden Road.

On the corner of Stable Hill see the unusual gargoyles on the end of the building near the Green Dragon and opposite, an old stone house dated 1730. Note the 'V' for Victory sign still legible on the brick wall, serving as a constant reminder of the end of war celebrations. On the next corner is The Pottery, which used to be a bakehouse and still has the original ovens.

Pass the Olde Three Cocks, a former coaching inn, and turn right into Farm Close, through a compact clutch of bungalows built on the site of a demolished farmhouse. Horseshoes form a unique 'New Inn' sign on the back gate of the one time pub. The timber yard is opposite, and the 4-storey 'Matchbox' looms ahead on the corner. Turn right into Old Dry Lane. The half hidden defunct reservoir is now overgrown, but used to store water, pumped up to supply local needs.

Cross the bypass with care, making a slight 'dog-leg', left and then right, to the lane next to Maltley Farm and proceed towards Fermyn Woods, where the golden leaves of beech remain through the winter. Norway spruce and Western red cedar comprise Harry's Park Wood.

Go forward over the cattle-grid, and nestled here are Bushylawn Lodge and Bungalows, surrounded by paddocks and plantations. In close proximity are the jumps which form part of the course of the annual Brigstock Horse Trials. The twisted and gnarled trunks of chestnut trees, avenues of oaks, sycamore and other broadleaf giants provide changing patterns all around Fermyn Woods Hall, barely visible among the trees.

Leaving the firm surface behind, not far from Bocase Farm, follow the waymark over the stile to a grass track on the edge of the woodland, which may be muddy in winter. Partially obscured by a fallen hawthorn is the Bocase Stone, about which many fanciful stories exist. You may be treading in the footsteps of Robin Hood!

From the gate follow the trail along the hedgerow and left into the old green lane, though no longer between the traditional double hedge. Re-enter the wood, with its plantations of Corsican pine which bear tawny cones with a sheen, different from the ovoid cones of the Scots pine.

Where the path diverges, follow the right fork to Meadow Leys and Old Dry Bushes, keeping an eye open for the secretive small muntjac or the fleet-of-foot fallow deer often found grazing in these more isolated parts. A gap in the hedge opens to fields and a panoramic view of the undulating countryside toward Geddington Chase, an important remnant of Rockingham Forest.

Over the stile and culvert, re-cross the bypass, going diagonally down the sloping bank, making for the path beside the Leylandii hedge and the disused water pumping station.

In the main street a salvaged plough enhances the forecourt of the private residence, formerly The New Inn, where the old hanging frame of the pub sign has been cleverly utilised.

Returning to the village, before making your way back to the park, follow the loop of roads which will take you through historic Brigstock. At the start of the High Street, a door in the archway next to the grocer's shop reveals a courtyard with the Barn Chapel at the far end.

On the corner of Bridge Street stands the solid Fotheringhay House, partly built with stone from the infamous castle. Opposite is The Olde Bakehouse, and below, dwellings converted from the old Angel public house. Horsebrook Cottage is self-explanatory, although horses no longer drink from the brook since the flow was diverted. The lovely stone bridge with its single cutwater remains above the delightful sunken garden, dotted about with graceful weeping willows and an elegant pond. Peeping over the parapet of the bridge over Harper's Brook, a tributory of the river Nene, the sound of water gurgling over the waterfall is music to the ears in this quiet lane. It is hard to imagine that the unique thatched Park Cottage was the very first factory here, prior to moving over to the 'Matchbox' on the other side of the village.

Continue along Park Walk, which has a well-placed commemorative bench, convenient to enjoy the vista of Harry's Park Wood and the manor house, secure in its niche in the hollow among the trees. On the right the dilapidated remains of a timber house are all that is left of the first timber yard before that business too moved to take its place in Back Lane.

Through the gateway of Hill Farm Herbs, another old farmhouse, the calf boxes and bull-pens have been converted to other uses. The brick Primitive Methodist chapel is here too, built in 1845, and now used by the local Women's Institute. Toward the bottom of the lane turn into Church Walk, going back over the brook, and admire the glorious sycamore tree in the corner of the graveyard. The parish church is well worth a visit.

Continue on through the heart of the village, Hall Hill, and into Mill Lane. Note The Manse and set back, the Congregational church (now the United Reformed church) built in 1799 — a simple building with a fine arched window. On the lower level the old watermill has been converted to private use and the waterwheel preserved.

Round the corner in Latham Street stands the School House of 1873 and the old Lathams Charity School, now in use for primary education. It was founded by the Rev. Nicholas Latimer of Barnwell and originally stood on the present site of the war memorial.

Now rejoin High Street and make your way back to the park by way of Stable Hill and Lyveden Road.

**Historical Notes**

**Fermyn Woods Hall** (Fermyn means 'farming') consists of a group of buildings built in the 14th century for use as a hunting lodge by the Head Archer.

**The Bocase Stone:** Located in Harry's Park Wood, the Bocase Stone is set, leaning, beside the footpath, marking the spot where stood the ancient Bocase Tree. It is inscribed 'In this plaes grew Bocase Tree' and, hardly legible, 'Here stood Bocase Tree'. Many stories have been related about that oak tree, the favourite telling of the legendary Robin Hood going to the church to pray on St Mary's Day. As he left with his followers, Sir Ralph de Manville and his men were lying in ambush. During the ensuing fight, an arrow flew through the church window and struck the priest who had betrayed him. Robin drew the enemy away from his men and flung his bow and arrows into the hollow Bocase Tree. It is also thought that archers in the forest would hang their bowcases here. A further explanation is that this is the place where Forest Courts were held in Saxon times.

**Brigstock:**

**The 'Matchbox'**, as it is affectionately nicknamed, no doubt because of its shape, is a symmetrical example of a classical Victorian mill, completed in 1873. Constructed of dressed Weldon stone, with cast iron windows, the façade has been perfectly restored to its original condition by the present occupants, after the cessation of use as a clothing factory.

**The parish church of St Andrew** is well-known for its notable Saxon tower, dating from AD 750-800 and crowned with a spire in the 14th century. It has a curious semi-circular extension, and a sundial under the gable of the porch. The church was burned down by the Danes but later rebuilt. It was added to in Norman times and further enlarged in 1133 when the monks of Cirencester took it over. The Lady Chapel is thought to have been gifted by Henry III in 1250. As with many church buildings, it is said to have a number of tunnels.

Inside lies the marble tomb of Robert Vernon, 1st Baron of Lyvden, who was Secretary of State at the outbreak of the Crimean War. The underground vault of the prominent Lyvden family, now sealed forever, is at the entrance to the churchyard.

**Hall Hill:** In the heart of the village, now designated a conservation area, a marker on the wall of Market House on Hall Hill proclaims 'Domesday Plaque 1086-1986'. This house was built by a construction known as 'cruck-frame', incorporating 2 tree trunks joined at the top. In 1466 Edward IV gave permission to hold a market on the Hill, and the Market Cross bears the dates and initials of the Queens of England from Elizabeth I.

Brigstock has long been the Boxing Day venue for the 'meet' of the Woodland Pytchley Hunt, and crowds of onlookers gather to see this colourful event on Hall Hill.

**The Manor House**, almost hidden from view down the driveway, was once in part a royal hunting lodge, the oldest section being the Great Hall going back to 1150. The house was occupied by Sir William Parr, Keeper of the Parks, in the 1520s. In 1602 Sir Robert Cecil, Earl of Salisbury, acquired the parks and illegally converted over 2,000 acres to agricultural cultivation, for which his family were later fined the sum of £20,000.

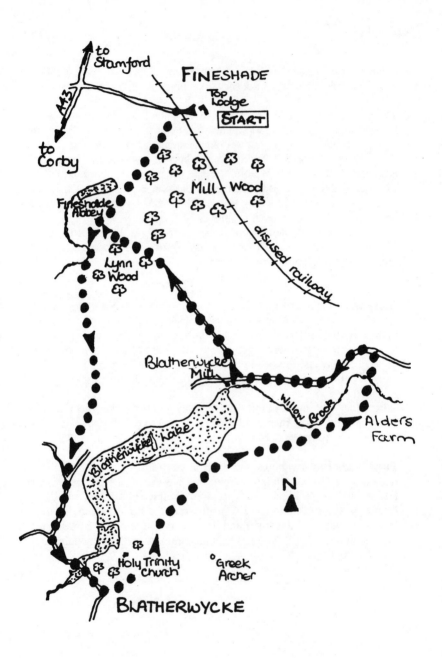

**Refreshments:** None at all en route. Public houses at Kings Cliffe, along the road from Blatherwycke, or the Royal Oak at Duddington, on the A43.

**How to get there:** The turning to Top Lodge, Fineshade, is to the east off the A43 Corby to Stamford road, about 6 miles south of the latter. Park at Top Lodge, Fineshade, in the car park.

**The Walk:** With your back to the buildings in the car park, walk to the right in the lane for a few yards, to the old brick bridge over the disused railway line. The express train service between Peterborough and Market Harborough of the London and North Western Railway ran through here. Opened in 1897, it had fallen into disuse by 1970. The cutting is now entirely swamped and overgrown by intense vegetation.

A fingerpost (which is sometimes turned off-course by pranksters) should point directly across the field, in line with the telegraph pole, and not on the woodland edge. The tallest tree, an ash, hangs over the stile in the far, thin hedge. Bear slightly to the right to follow the path through the trees. This weaves along the side of the hill and is fairly enclosed, until it reaches the gate at the bottom into a field.

Here, the vista widens to another little valley and in front, part of the old Georgian mansion, are the stables and lake of Fineshade Abbey. The notices on the fencing are reminders that this is private property and therefore out of bounds, interesting though it may be!

The waymark directs one up and over the hill on a straight course, keeping the woods to the left, going toward the brook. Look over to the rather bleak frontage of Laxton Hall, built prior to 1811, and the elaborate lodges and gateway on the A43 to the right.

Do not cross the brook, but pass through a cattle-pen (which may be temporary) and up the hill again, in a diagonal line, to the far side of the brow, now more gentle. In the distance is the historic town of Stamford.

Another, broader valley is now in sight, so follow the waymarks over the fields to descend and join the lane, at the Wakerley turn, which continues to the village of Blatherwycke, hugging one end of the lake (also private).

# WALK SEVEN

# Fineshade and Blatherwycke

**Introduction:** This is a walk through tranquil woodland, once a part of vast, ancient Rockingham Forest, which is well documented as the domain for the sport of Kings, hunting. Deer still range these quiet areas undisturbed, and may be seen if come upon in silence. The path traverses a series of small, compact valleys, gradually opening up to the site of Fineshade Abbey, founded originally in the early 13th century.

The pastoral hills and hollows in turn bring the walker to the slumbering old village of Blatherwycke. Beside it, the man-made lake is an ideal spot for birdwatching (from the outside of the boundary wall, please) and serene reflection. You might also wish to make a short side trip to visit the mysterious Greek Archer.

The return bridleway separates 2 woods, planted with a selection of familiar trees. The Norway Spruce, our traditional Christmas tree, with long, pendulous cones, is there, intermixed with the soft-needled Douglas Fir, an extensively planted and important forest tree providing valuable timber, and the evergreen Lawson Cypress, a hardy and tolerant tree bearing round cones and flattened scale-like leaves, which is also grown as a timber crop.

Top Lodge, liberally cloaked by trees, is the central office of the Forestry Commission, comprising an attractive cluster of stone buildings with Collyweston slate roofs, formerly a farm. The wall enclosed the old farmyard and cattle-pens, now sensitively renovated with native materials in this isolated setting.

**Distance:** About 9 miles in all, but a shorter circuit from Blatherwycke Bridge, round the lake and back along the lane would be a pleasant stroll of approximately 5 miles. This is Forestry Commission land and walkers are asked to keep to marked paths and keep dogs under control at all times. OS Landranger 1:50,000 Sheet 141.

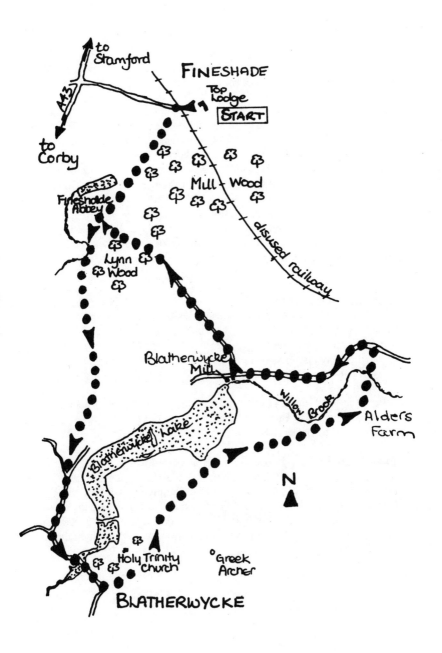

windows, the façade has been perfectly restored to its original condition by the present occupants, after the cessation of use as a clothing factory.

**The parish church of St Andrew** is well-known for its notable Saxon tower, dating from AD 750-800 and crowned with a spire in the 14th century. It has a curious semi-circular extension, and a sundial under the gable of the porch. The church was burned down by the Danes but later rebuilt. It was added to in Norman times and further enlarged in 1133 when the monks of Cirencester took it over. The Lady Chapel is thought to have been gifted by Henry III in 1250. As with many church buildings, it is said to have a number of tunnels.

Inside lies the marble tomb of Robert Vernon, 1st Baron of Lyvden, who was Secretary of State at the outbreak of the Crimean War. The underground vault of the prominent Lyvden family, now sealed forever, is at the entrance to the churchyard.

**Hall Hill:** In the heart of the village, now designated a conservation area, a marker on the wall of Market House on Hall Hill proclaims 'Domesday Plaque 1086-1986'. This house was built by a construction known as 'cruck-frame', incorporating 2 tree trunks joined at the top. In 1466 Edward IV gave permission to hold a market on the Hill, and the Market Cross bears the dates and initials of the Queens of England from Elizabeth I.

Brigstock has long been the Boxing Day venue for the 'meet' of the Woodland Pytchley Hunt, and crowds of onlookers gather to see this colourful event on Hall Hill.

**The Manor House**, almost hidden from view down the driveway, was once in part a royal hunting lodge, the oldest section being the Great Hall going back to 1150. The house was occupied by Sir William Parr, Keeper of the Parks, in the 1520s. In 1602 Sir Robert Cecil, Earl of Salisbury, acquired the parks and illegally converted over 2,000 acres to agricultural cultivation, for which his family were later fined the sum of £20,000.

The single street, lined by a mix of old and renovated dwellings mingling happily together, meanders down to the ancient bridge, which has 2 deep cutwaters, spanning the water and extensive reedbeds overhung by a profusion of trees and shrubs. Pass the gatehouse and deserted grounds of the former Hall, which is no longer in existence, to the bend at the top of the short incline, to the sign 'Blatherwycke Church'. Turn left into a gateless gap to the bridleway, next to a mossy roofed barn, staying close to the boundary railing.

Take a brief detour to the curious statue of the Greek Archer, lonely and forlorn and totally incongruous in the middle of a field, encircled by a dilapidated wooden fence. He was, perhaps, a centre-piece in the formal Hall gardens.

Continue forward, at first parallel with the lake, then leaving it behind, crossing 2 fields and making for Alders Farm. Left here on the track, over Willow Brook, and left again onto the little road to the mill, an austere place, now sadly derelict, which has miraculously managed to retain its elegant, arched windows. It is a pleasant place to take a break, to sit by the tranquil lake and listen to the birdsong and the buzz of insects in summer. Or perch by the race and weir, the water dashing and splashing as it slides away over the rapids.

Opposite the opening are sheds used for agricultural purposes, and to one side of these a bridleway proceeds along a hard track to the woodland. Keep to the path as it curves to the left, which marks the boundary between Lynn Wood and Mill Wood, the latter planted in 1957. Emerge to a hilly field within sight of Fineshade Abbey, and return to the start of the walk by Top Lodge by the outward route.

## Historical Notes

**Blatherwycke:** The prominent family here was the Staffords, who married into the O'Briens, and their emblem, with interlaced initials and a lovers' knot signifying the uniting of the two households, is still evident on the older cottages and on the stone bridge. One of their descendants, Sir Humphrey Stafford, built the grand Kirby Hall not far away. It was ultimately completed by Sir Christopher Hatton, an ardent Royalist, who was also involved in the construction of Holdenby House.

The Hall, built in 1713, replacing an older house, was demolished in 1948 as a result of devastation by a succession of troops and prisoners of war during the Second World War. Two spinster O'Brien sisters lived to witness the final indignity of the Hall, where they had lived for 50 years. They had retired to a wooden bungalow erected in the kitchen garden. Their brother, Major Egerton O'Brien, who lived in County Clare, sold the Hall for £1,600. It was demolished and the resulting stone was used for further building elsewhere. The stable block, however, has survived and has been converted to commercial use.

The gardens, now silent and hopelessly tangled, draw the walker keen on solitude into this neglected wilderness. The enormous lake was dug by Irish labourers, said to have been brought over to this country by the O'Briens at the period of the potato famine in Ireland. It is thought to be the largest man-made lake in this county, and was a source of water for the ironworks at Corby in its heyday.

**The church of the Holy Trinity** is close by in the grounds, standing on a knoll, with a Norman tower and small west doorway. The modern stained glass window, in clear colours, depicts Our Lord in the role of shepherd, cradling a lamb. Fine memorials are inside, dedicated to the Staffords and Sir Humphrey in particular, who died in 1548. There is also one by Thomas Randolph, a poet, commissioned by Sir Christopher Hatton. On an inscribed tablet of 1640, an intriguing poem commences 'Here sleepe thirteene together in one tombe', and proceeds to tell a tale.

On the edge of the graveyard, a back to front headstone for Anthony Williams, who died in 1836, is comparatively well preserved and legible. He was a black man who rescued his master from drowning in the lake, it is recorded, although his final demise seems to be lost in the vagaries of local knowledge.

**Fineshade Abbey:** This was the site of pre-Roman iron workings. Then the castle of Hely, or Hymel, graced this lovely hillside, before the foundation of a monastery in the early 13th century. It was deserted and demolished at the commencement of John's reign, and visible earthworks exist. When Richard Engayne founded the priory for Augustinian canons, to the north of the castle, it was known as the Priory of Fineshed. The founder endowed the prior with lands at Blatherwycke and Laxton. It eventually passed to Sir Robert Kirkham, who converted it into a residence which was destroyed in 1749.

The Georgian mansion that came next was demolished as unsafe in 1956. Late 18th century stables still stand, with a dome over the entrance, creating a decorative feature.

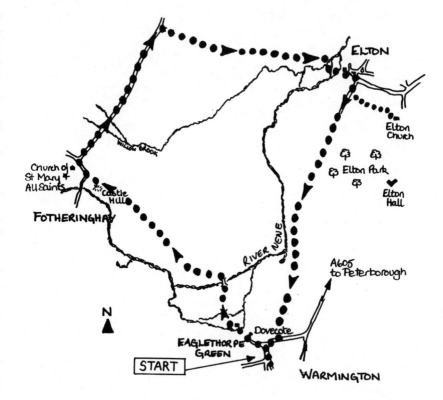

ELTON

Elton Church

Elton Park

Elton Hall

Church of St Mary & All Saints

Wilson Brook

Castle Hill

FOTHERINGHAY

RIVER NENE

A605 to Peterborough

N

Dovecote

EAGLETHORPE GREEN

START

WARMINGTON

# Warmington, Eaglethorpe Green, Fotheringhay and Elton

**Introduction:** Fotheringhay is a well-known and much loved corner of Northamptonshire and draws visitors like a magnet. The poignant story of the imprisonment and subsequent tragic death of Mary, Queen of Scots, attracts people from all walks of life. This tranquil setting was once part of the vast royal Rockingham Forest, and the lush Nene Valley provided the necessary winter fodder for the prolific herds of deer.

The striking church of St Mary and All Saints, crowning the rise like a cathedral from its idyllic position on the banks of the river Nene, may be seen as a landmark for miles around, inviting the traveller to take a closer look. Nearby only a grim collection of stones from Fotheringhay Castle remain on their grassy knoll, yet they are enough to evoke vibrant memories of the past. This stimulating walk also takes you to a picturesque ruined mill, through water meadows and over the lovely river Nene.

**Distance:** The complete circuit is about 5½ miles, or 3 miles from Warmington to Fotheringhay and return. Allow 2½ hours for exploration of the area, or a little over 1 hour for the latter. OS Landranger 1:50,000 Sheet 142.

**Refreshments:** The only public house immediately en route is the Red Lion at the beginning of the walk. Other pubs at Fotheringhay and Elton are near the route of the walk.

**How to get there:** Warmington village has more than 1 turning off the A605 Oundle to Peterborough road. A good bus service operates on this route.

**The Walk:** Park in Warmington village, which is rather spread out and has many attractive houses fashioned from stone quarried at Barnack. Taking care on the severe bend, follow the road out of Warmington to the tiny hamlet of Eaglethorpe Green, graced by handsome mellowed stone houses and giving a hint of the pleasures to come!

In the paddock adjacent to Eaglethorpe Farm stands a circular dovecote, and further down the lane was the site of Peterborough Abbey, Burystead Manor and the Chapel of St Andrew, all long since gone.

The sound of rushing, gushing water heralds the now derelict Warmington Mill, the site first recorded here as a working mill in the Domesday Book (1086). Follow the Nene Way waymark around the front of this gaunt place and over the sluice, which runs beneath your feet into a dark pool surrounded by a stand of poplars. Go left alongside the race and over the stile, going away from the boats moored on the back-water.

Traverse the sprawling water-meadows (liable to flood in winter) and cross the lock and weir over the river. The disused railway track is barely noticeable as the path goes up to old ridge and furrow pastures. The high lantern tower of the glorious church at Fotheringhay beckons over the skyline and there is a sight of Tansor, almost hidden among the trees, to the left.

Keeping to the fenceline, note the twisted hawthorn trees, then over the stile to the farmyard. Past the sheds, clamber over or around the bosky Castle Hill to see the meagre remains of Fotheringhay Castle, which in its heyday commanded a wide view of the river and the ancient bridge.

The Nene Way exits at Garden Farm (and is left behind at this point), which incorporates a worn Gothic arch, also of historical interest. Take time to visit the church of St Mary and All Saints before turning into the Nassington-Yarwell road opposite the gates. Go over the 2 bridges of Willow Brook and up the hill for about 1 mile to where a fingerpost on each side of the road indicates the path.

Turn right next to the oak tree, down the track and along the top of a deep drainage ditch. Make for the footbridge over the main river (this may be obscured by crops in certain seasons) and cross the bridge and sluicegate. From Elton Mill, forward to Middle Street and right into Chapel Lane, passing charming dwellings with tidy, netted thatched roofs and intriguing gateways and courtyards. At the last house an easy detour over 2 fields may be taken to Elton church, prominent on the horizon. The quiet graveyard has ancient sentinel yews towering over the leaning, mossy headstones.

Returning to Chapel Lane, continue on this pastoral walk to Elton Park, through an iron gate, keeping to the right of the fence and over the rise to the bridge. Up the slope toward the trees, pause to look back at stately Elton Hall (entrance from the A605), and to the right through the trees catch a brief glimpse of Fotheringhay church and the winding river Nene.

Go through the gate to the path along the escarpment, where the sound of an occasional boat passing out of sight below may be heard through dense vegetation. Emerge to a field headland on the woodland edge, where the broach spire of Warmington church, begun in the 12th century, lies ahead.

At the next gate, stay to the right of the fence down to the main road and fingerpost 'Bridleway to Ecton'. Use the gravel path for safety around the bend back to Warmington where the walk began.

## Historical Notes

**Eaglethorpe Green:** Although recorded as a medieval hamlet, this tiny collection of houses is all that remains after depopulation in the 16th century. The fascinating circular stone dovecote next to Eaglethorpe Farm was built in the 18th century and contains 797 nesting boxes. It is now scheduled as an Ancient Monument.

**Fotheringhay:** Fotheringhay is listed in the Domesday Book as 'Fodringeai' and mentioned as early as 1060. The name means 'enclosure', which would have been appropriate at the time when Rockingham Forest covered these parts. The octagonal lantern tower of the church guided travellers to safety, offering protection from the robbers and assassins who roamed at will.

Over the centuries, 2 castles have graced this spot on the bank of the river Nene. A pathetic pile of stones, the mound and the vestige of a moat are all that now remain to mark this historic site. The first castle was built here in about 1100 for Simon de Senlis, Earl of Northampton and Huntingdon, who married the daughter of Judith, niece of the

Conqueror. This was rebuilt in the 14th century by Edmund de Langley, fifth son of Edward III, founder of the House of York. He began to build a college attached to the church around 1370, which was continued by his son and founded in 1411. After the Dissolution of the Monasteries this was demolished by the Duke of Northumberland along with parts of the church, leaving the truncated church building as it appears today.

Richard III was born in the castle in 1452 and was the last English king to die in battle. His parents, Richard Plantagenet and Cecily Neville, were Duke and Duchess of York. Members of their families were buried in the church and commemorated in a stained glass window.

The remnants of the castle are now (hopefully) preserved for posterity, and record the place where Mary, Queen of Scots was beheaded in the Great Hall. She was brought to Fotheringhay Castle in September 1586 after being held captive in prisons up and down the country for 18 years, and was finally executed on 8th February 1587 at the age of 44 years. Her heart was removed and buried in the grounds of the castle, and her body sealed in a lead coffin until it was carried to Peterborough Cathedral. Her embalmed torso rested there until 1612 when it was moved to Westminster Abbey to lie with other royal personages.

Her son, James I (VI of Scotland) succeeded Elizabeth in 1603, finally uniting the crowns of England and Scotland, and it is thought that he razed the castle where his mother had perished. A patch of Scottish thistles may still be seen growing on Castle Hill in summer, purported to have survived from those stormy days.

Garden Farm, originally the New Inn hostelry, built by Edward IV, incorporates a Gothic arch. The inn was used to accommodate the overflow of visitors to the castle, and is likely to have housed the Queen's executioner, Bull, in the room above the arch.

The first bridge was constructed of timber in 1330, downstream from the present site, and later rebuilt at a cost of £180 by order of Queen Elizabeth in 1573. In 1722 the current handsome bridge of 4 arches was built of stone quarried from Kings Cliffe.

**St Mary and All Saints** dominates the landscape, standing high on the river bank. It is said that medieval music is sometimes heard emanating from the lofty interior when it is assumed to be empty!

The approach to the porch is along a short avenue of young lime trees, and the elegant flying buttresses, tall windows and noble proportions combine to effect this most striking monument. This dazzling church, with its fine oak pulpit, mass of windows, soaring roof and delicate vaulting in the bell tower, reflects the major role it has played in our history.

**Elton:** Elton Hall fills a site which has been occupied since the Norman Conquest, standing in 200 acres of unspoilt parkland. It is now a treasure trove of fine furniture and early 15th century paintings. The library contains Henry VIII's prayer book and other rare volumes. There is also a state coach on display, which was used in Queen Victoria's Jubilee celebrations. The Hall is open in summer at selected times only.

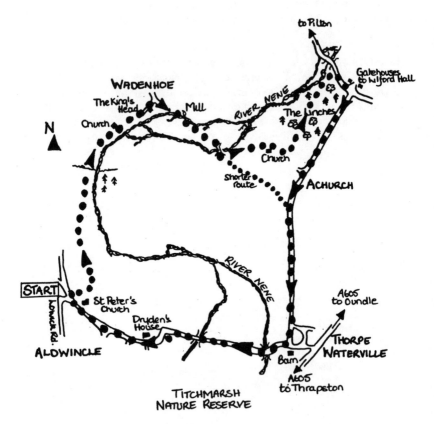

to Pilton

Gatehouses to Lilford Hall

WADENHOE

The King's Head

Mill

Church

RIVER NENE

The Linches

N

Church

Shorter route

ACHURCH

RIVER NENE

START

A605 to Oundle

St Peter's Church

Dryden's House

THORPE WATERVILLE

ALDWINCLE

Lonner Rd.

Barn

A605 to Thrapston

TITCHMARSH NATURE RESERVE

# Aldwincle, Wadenhoe, Thorpe Achurch and Thorpe Waterville

**Introduction:** The lovely villages of Aldwincle, Wadenhoe, the tiny hamlet of Thorpe Achurch, and Thorpe Waterville have a special appeal, linked by the fabulous scenery. The birthplace of the poet John Dryden is just one of the discoveries to be made on this exhilarating walk. The first half of the walk follows the Nene Way, and this particular stretch is a delight. The broad valley of the river Nene is rich in archaeological heritage and totally absorbing to the naturalist.

The route borders the Titchmarsh Nature Reserve and Heronry, owned and managed by the Northants Wildlife Trust. A constant magnet to bird-watchers, the property embraces 180 acres, where visitors are requested to keep to marked paths and refrain from entering the wood where herons nest. It is located between Thrapston and Aldwincle (access from Lowick Road) and lies at the centre of a large tract of gravel pits. It is, of course, a very sensitive area, and needs to be treated as such, and perhaps the interested walker might care to take along a pair of binoculars and observe the lakes from a distance.

It is a haven for birds, free from the pressures of fishing and sailing, with hides accessible by arrangement. Islands provide nesting sites for the common tern, and migrating waders take full advantage of the muddy shores. Ducks, coots and other residents overwinter on the lake. Several rare species have been attracted to this sanctuary, which also harbours a myriad of insects, wildlife, flora and fauna.

**Distance:** The walk is about 6 miles in a circular route, the shorter version 2 miles less, and will take roughly 3 hours at 'ambler's pace'.
OS Landranger 1:50,000 Sheet 141.

**Refreshments:** The King's Head at Wadenhoe is an old inn built of local limestone, with birds' nests under the eaves and spacious grounds sweeping down to the river. The Fox Inn at Thorpe Waterville is situated on the corner of the Aldwincle Road and the main road (A605).

**How to get there:** Aldwincle is off the A605 Thrapston to Oundle road, turning at Thorpe Waterville, and has street parking only.

**The Walk:** Starting in the main street of the spread out village of Aldwincle, look for St Peter's church, standing back from the bordering wall, where the first signpost 'Nene Way' appears. The next wooden stile leads between the gardens of the new rectory and a hedge, behind which lie a small cluster of new country homes, to a third stile.

Turn sharp left here along the headland of 2 fields (hedge to the left, then hedge to the right), with sweeping views down to the river Nene, over meadows and undulating rural tranquillity. In the distance, the spire of Achurch church peeps from the trees.

Continuing downhill, the path stays close to Boathouse Spinney, where several impressive redwoods tower above their lesser neighbours, to stout double stiles, linked by a planked bridge with handrails over the stream. Go up the slope, through a section designated as a Site of Special Scientific Interest, where, in summer, the spectacular banded demoiselle damselflies flit for the brief period of their lives among the reeds and rushes.

The wooded area ahead has been known since the 15th century as Conygher (with many spelling variations, meaning 'rabbit warren'). Tantalising glimpses of the river now, opening to a glade of tall ash trees, where a handy felled trunk thoughtfully fashioned into a seat makes a useful resting place. Pick up the Way again, treading secured sleepers over trickling springs, to the next field.

The church of St Michael and All Angels at Wadenhoe stands high on the hill of old grassland, and is well worth a visit, or even a further pause on the seat overlooking the peaceful scenery. Very early in the springtime this path is edged by a string of bright crocuses, to cheer the breeziest day. Sounds of water herald the weir and locks below, and already the pretty village is in sight. Welcome refreshment may be obtained at The King's Head, with riverside lawns and magnificent willows with gnarled trunks of the most subtle hues. There are often assorted boats moored on these banks, as it is a popular stop-over for both river and land travellers.

Leaving the pub behind, walk up the hill and right at the T-junction into Mill Lane, admiring the host of ancient trees in the grounds of Wadenhoe House, now in use as a Conference Centre. A circular dovecote still stands in the stable-yard, containing 500 lath and plaster nesting boxes.

As the lane curves down to the river, the picturesque Mill House stands back in splendour, close to the watercourse, rich in aquatic species, where in the old days carts and animals would ford the water. Go under the spreading chestnut tree and over the white bridge, taking a moment to lean against the rail and savour the scene, where graceful swans are usually in sight. From here, go diagonally away from this quiet backwater, across the meadow, making for the high river bridge (to allow for boat traffic) and cross it, to the stile in the corner of the field ahead.

For the shorter route, bear sharp right after this stile, to follow a public right of way directly uphill, emerging behind a farmyard, and exit to the Achurch-Thorpe Waterville road.

To continue forward, make for the opposite corner, where 2 mighty chestnut trees appear like sentinels in the pasture, to the lower entrance of the graveyard of the church of John the Baptist, where the path departs through a magnificent porch lychgate. Go past the iron lamp-posts and gate leading to the Old Rectory, along the empty lane to the Nene Way post at the entrance to The Linches.

In this pretty, private woodland be sure to keep to the riding, turning left at the first intersection and a flight of well laid steps to enter the wood. Sounds of the river rise up the escarpment, eventually disclosing a lock and buildings. Exit right here on the Pilton to Lilford road.

Up the steep hill now to the twin gatehouses of Lilford Park and Hall and turn right, departing from the Nene Way. An unusual box hedge banks the wide grass verge. At certain times of the year, toads lie like dried leather patches on this road — a tragedy of the breeding season in these parts, when they are returning to their natural spawning grounds.

The tidy hamlet of Thorpe Achurch has a neat War Memorial and lovingly restored cottages, with real country gardens, and an old well-head with a carved canopy in memory of a member of the local prominent

Powys family. Beside Rectory Farm, a fingerpost indicates the point where the short-cut rejoins the circuit.

Down the long sloping road now, the lovely countryside stretching away like a patchwork quilt, with half-hidden villages appearing mysterious and beckoning. The facing barn at Thorpe Waterville appears to have 2 staring eyes casting baleful looks at the approaching traveller! Right at the T-junction and into the lane toward Aldwincle, crossing The Staunch and river bridge. Across the lakes can be seen the Titchmarsh Nature Reserve. The road here has a raised wall topped by a high bank, as this section was susceptible to flooding, which is now useful for an elevated assessment of the scenery.

Just after Brancey Bridge, seek out a stile in the hedgerow to the left, which eliminates a nasty bend in the road. Take a diagonal path, leaving the field beneath venerable trees near to All Saints' church, almost opposite the former rectory, now Dryden House, birthplace of John Dryden, the poet. The inauguration of a Pocket Park, a spinney rescued from sure ruin if left unattended, now provides a secluded corner for wildlife.

The long main street of Aldwincle has many fine stone houses, with garden walls frequently bedecked with lichens and mosses. It will bring you back to your starting point.

## Historical Notes

**Aldwincle:** The Domesday Book of 1086 lists Aldwincle as 'Eldewincle', relating to 'nook' or 'old corner'. Two medieval churches, St Peter's with its elegant broach spire, and All Saints', with a bell tower, were built by rival lords of the manor, each with their own parish priest. The latter, dating from the 13th century, fell into disuse and became redundant, but is still kept in good order. The 15th century brass depicting William de Aldwyncle, with his wife and dog, remains here. The estate eventually passed to Lord Lilford, who became owner of both manors. There was also an endowed school, free to the children of both parishes, when they were ultimately united.

Early settlement remains lie close to All Saints' church, where the foundations of stone buildings and quantities of pottery have been retrieved over the years.

**John Dryden**, the writer, poet, satirist and playwright, later to become Poet Laureate to Charles II, was born in 1631 at the former rectory, renamed Dryden House. Although among the lesser gentry, his parents both bore titles, as was the mode of the day. They were not residents of the village, travelling here for the birth of their child, but his maternal grandfather was rector here. Dryden died in May 1700.

**Wadenhoe:** Situated on the north bank of the river Nene, Wadenhoe must rank high among the wealth of pretty villages in this county. The old Saxon word for ford, 'waden' and 'hoe', a hill, were combined to create this descriptive name, though the spelling has varied through the centuries.

The manor of Wadenhoe was held by Alberious of Constance and valued at £3, prior to the Norman conquest. Thereafter passing eventually in 1551 to Sir Walter Mildmay, later the estate came into the family of Thomas Hunt, whose descendants, Carol and Thomas Welch-Hunt were brutally murdered by bandits whilst on their honeymoon in Italy in 1824.

The Right Honourable George Ward-Hunt, who later inherited the estate, was Chancellor of the Exchequer in Disraeli's Cabinet in 1868, in addition to being First Lord of the Admiralty. The first telegraph in any village in England was installed here, so that he could be kept in touch with Government affairs. He was also responsible for building the gasworks in 1869, on the site of the present village hall, providing lighting for the streets and dwellings.

A stone dated 1653 at the rear of Manor Farm House, indicates the oldest house in the village. A similar stone at Wadenhoe House is dated 1657, where a circular limestone dovecote survives in the stable-yard, with a roof of Collyweston slate.

**The church of St Michael and All Angels** stands on the hilltop above the river, with a saddleback tower dating back to Norman times, and is set apart from the present village. It is thought that the original medieval settlement near to the church disappeared as a result of the plague in the 17th century. Castle Close was a likely site for a castle or fortified manor, though no mention of one exists.

The church contains interesting memorials and stained glass windows, dedicated to members of local eminent families. These include the Ward-Hunt forebears, Sir Michael Culme-Seymour and his wife, whose descendants now occupy Rockingham Castle, as well as the parish schoolmistress. The ringing chamber, with Royal Arms, crest and shield, houses 6 bells. The altar, pulpit and handsome offertory bags, all have intriguing historical connections.

**Mill House**, now privately owned, was built on the site of an earlier mill, recorded in the Domesday Book.

**The Linches:** The Linches, or Lynches, means 'uncultivated places' or escarpment.

**Lilford Hall and Park:** Lilford Hall, built in 1635, is a listed Jacobean place of merit, with a park of some 240 acres. It came into the possession of the Powys family in 1711. One of their descendants was created Lord Lilford in 1797, and the estate remained in their hands for several generations. The fourth Baron Lilford was President of the British Ornithologists Union from 1867 and created the famous aviaries. These have now been restored and house native and exotic birds. He also introduced Little Owls to Britain in the 1890s.

**Thorpe Achurch:** Both Iron Age and Roman settlements have been identified in the vicinity of the present dwellings, discernible from the air by crop-marks over Cornbrash (a layer of thin limestone of the Oolite and Upper Jurassic period, often mixed with sand or clay). The Roman way from Water Newton to Irchester passed close to the existing road.

**The Church of St John the Baptist** dominates the lonely graveyard, which has many ancient headstones. The spire, tower and chancel were built in the 13th century by a knight, Ascelone de Waterville. The fine marble monument in the south transept is of Sir Thomas Powys, who died in 1719, was brought here after the demolition of the church at Lilford. The impressive carved oak canopy over the lychgate bears a further inscription.

**Thorpe Waterville:** This is an early Danish settlement. All that remains of the castle or fortified manor are the walls of a lofty banqueting hall, with a pair of circular windows and a chimneybreast, resembling a face from the outside. The rest is said to have been destroyed in the Wars of the Roses. It is now in use as a barn.

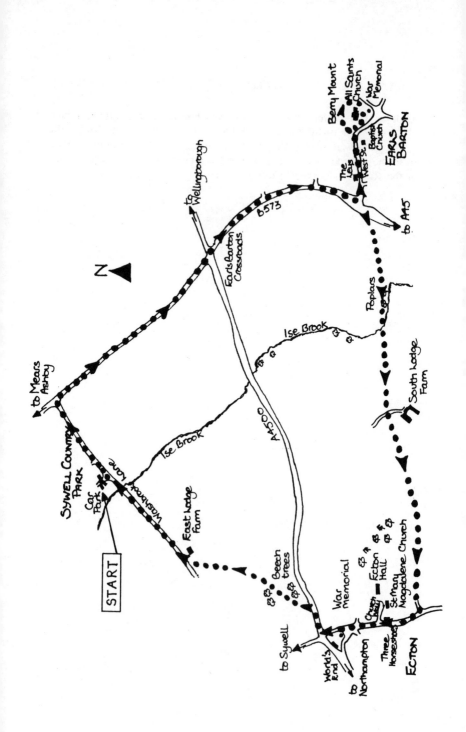

# Earls Barton and Ecton

**Introduction:** Sywell Country Park is an attractive place from which to begin this walk, as there are so many amenities on offer here. Indeed, you might feel you need go no further, but a stroll around the reservoir ensures a good stretch for the legs and the walk embraces 2 villages, Earls Barton and Ecton. Both are completely different and of great historical importance as Roman and Anglo-Saxon settlements, being prominently placed on the north side of the river Nene, which used to be a trade highway. The former has progressed and expanded by virtue of trade, particularly the Northamptonshire speciality of shoemaking, but in contrast the little village of Ecton, with connections to the Franklin family, has remained intact and is now designated a conservation area. This quiet place, laced with history, lies nestled unobtrusively among the trees, within sight of the county town. Wonderful views over the surrounding countryside provide a further incentive to discover this delightful area.

**Distance:** About 5 miles, taking roughly 2 hours with time to stop and stare! OS Landranger 1:50,000 Sheet 152.

**Refreshments:** There are a number of public houses and shops in Earls Barton. Ecton has 2 pubs, the Three Horseshoes and the World's End.

**How to get there:** Sywell Country Park is located 1 mile to the north-east of the A4500 Northampton to Wellingborough road, turning at the crossroads at Earls Barton into the Mears Ashby road, and signed left into Washbrook Lane. A regular bus service operates between the 2 towns.

**The Walk:** Leaving the main gates of the Park, turn left up the hill to the T-junction, and right, past a row of detached houses, to the traffic lights at Earls Barton crossroads (A4500). Cross straight over and keep to the pavement to West Street (garage on corner).

Turn left into West Street, where ahead the ancient Saxon tower of the parish church of All Saints fills the view, passing 'The Leys', built in the 17th century and formerly a farmhouse. The raised and railed path continues down to the Green.

The churchyard has bushy yews among the gravestones, and the deep church porch with zigzag stonework over the massive doors, opens to a lofty interior. The War Memorial, on a lower level, stands above the Green, where a pot-pourri of shops lie scattered around this hub of the village. Adjacent to the church is Berry Mount, said to have been a Norman motte and bailey castle, beside a curved ditch ringed by trees.

Retracing your steps, the Baptist church, built in 1785, and the 17th and 18th century farmhouse, are among the miscellany of old buildings in this street.

At the corner, bear slightly to the left, crossing to the far side of the B573 (Northampton to Mears Ashby road), to a fingerpost in the hedgerow 'Bridleway to Ecton', noting the farmer's request to keep dogs on a lead. From this point, a panoramic view of the Nene Valley stretches away, dotted about with patchwork fields, farmhouses and barns, with Cogenhoe on the far slope.

Walk down the pasture toward a spinney of uniform poplars and over the stile, to the wooden bridge over the Ise Brook, and uphill, where 3 big oaks occupy an isolated position. Cross the lane which leads to South Lodge Farm, through a kissing-gate, where the footpath is usually defined. More sweeping valley vistas, including the hamlet and handsome banded stone church of St Mary at Whiston, nestled against the hill. (Did you know that the origin of 'kissing-gate' is believed to have come from the notion of the gate 'kissing' the 2 posts — and not the more romantic one?).

Soon Ecton comes into sight, where the mellowed stone wall overhung with trees marks the boundary of Ecton Hall, with its magnificent facade affording a glimpse of elegant conservatories and courtyards. The square tower of the church, with gargoyles and a weathervane on each of the 4 corners, is shyly revealed among the tree-tops. Rising from the skyline of distant Northampton, directly ahead, rears the Express Lift Tower, locally nicknamed 'The Lighthouse'.

Into the dip and over the rise, the path joins Barton Fields, and merges with the High Street, facing a row of red brick cottages with fancy woodwork, dated 1896. Bear to the right, where beautiful stone walls on either side are a joy to behold, as are the majority of dwellings. Fitted snugly into an outer wall is an arched gateway bearing the sign 'Staff Only' — a reminder of a very different society?

The Three Horseshoes pub butts onto the street, with high dormer windows, and opposite, Wheelwright's Cottage is typical of its type. The cottages with low doorways have been tastefully restored by craftsmen, enabling traditional stone dwellings to retain the character of this conservation village. Even the inevitable newer houses are in keeping with this treasured style and coach-lamps, lanterns and lamp-posts enhance secluded doorways and alleys, and there are real old-fashioned gardens. Tucked away in a small courtyard stands the 'school for poor children' built by John Palmer in the 17th century.

The walker might like to dally awhile in Church Way, to enjoy the tranquillity and admire the grand Ecton House and Ecton Hall, the latter with an imposing pillared gateway topped by stone spheres. The church of St Mary Magdalene enhances this peaceful corner of traditional England at its best, with a porch lantern and moss-bedecked headstones.

Walk past Blacksmith's Yard to the road fork, and at Parsons Close there are curious street level arches in the wall, lined with brick. At the apex, the unusual War Memorial is inscribed 'Ecton is not unmindful'. Here now too is the World's End pub, with historical associations with the Battle of Naseby.

Go to the right for a short distance on the curving incline of the path beside the A4500, making for a line of beech trees on the horizon. Cross to the 'Footpath' sign, skirting the holly hedge to an avenue of splendid smooth-trunked giant beeches, and to one side (on the road) is a quaint little gatehouse. Follow the path diagonally over 2 fields to East Lodge in Washbrook Lane.

At the foot of the hill, next to Sywell Country Park, the patch around the abandoned sheepwash has been restored and a seat thoughtfully placed to provide a restful corner near the brook. You can now return to the car park or your walk may be extended by 2½ miles by traversing the perimeter of the reservoir.

## Historical Notes

**Earls Barton:** Aerial evidence from cropmarks indicates enclosures, pits and ditches. Iron Age coins and Roman pottery, flints and tiles have been recovered from scattered sites in this area, where there are wide gravel terraces, overlaid by sand and limestone.

The highest point, Round Hill, was an important part of the old Saxon kingdom of Mercia. Berry Mount, ovoid and flat topped, is bounded by a wide ditch, and thought to be part of an ancient motte and bailey castle and possible site of an Iron Age hill fort.

Millenium celebrations were held in 1970 for the Saxon tower of the church of All Saints, which replaced the wooden structure destroyed by the Danes in AD 860. The fluted screen decorated with painted butterflies is a relatively recent innovation in this massive building of solid stone walls. A descendant of the family of Earl Simon de Senlis the Younger is credited with the Norman elements of this edifice.

The village is recorded in the Domesday Book of 1086 as 'Bartone', and Countess Judith, niece of the Conqueror, is named as the land and mill owner, whose father-in-law had become the Earl of Northampton in 1065.

Earls Barton's prosperity was centred upon the growing of grain until the 14th and 15th centuries, when sheep farming came to the fore. The production of woollen cloth then followed, until an industrial change occurred and the craft of weaving baskets, mats and other goods gained favour, utilising the prolific supply of rushes from the river valley.

Shoes were made as early as the 13th century, and soon the tanning of leather was introduced and the production of footwear developed into a major industry, which continues to this day. As a result of this the population increased enormously, resulting in a modern, thriving community.

The origin of the custom of eating Leek Pie on Shrove Tuesday is shrouded in mystery (the locals are known affectionately as 'Barton Leeks'). There is a tale of a chaff cutter being deployed on the Green to chop the leeks, and the women gathering round to catch the pieces in their coarse aprons. The vegetables were then taken home to be made into pies, and carried to one of the several bakehouses in the village to be cooked.

**Ecton:** Late Iron Age pottery, cobbles and cattle bones have been unearthed along this ridge, also Roman kilns and pottery, coins, jewellery, flints and fragments of roof tiles. The name Ecton is said to date back to Anglo Saxon times, and was recorded in the Domesday Book as 'Eckingstone'. After the Norman conquest, the manor of Ecton came into the Montgomery family.

The common fields of the parish were enclosed by an Act of Parliament in 1759. Vestiges of the old ridge and furrow pastures remain.

**The Three Horseshoes** pub was built on the site of the original smithy, which had belonged to the ancestors of Benjamin Franklin, the American statesman. They had owned a farm and a bell-foundry for 300 years, where the bells for Lichfield Cathedral were cast.

Josia Franklin emigrated to Boston, USA, in 1682. His son Benjamin was born in 1706, and was to become a writer, inventor, scientist and one of the Founding Fathers, along with George Washington. This gifted man founded the University of Pennsylvania, organised a postal service and a lending library, and worked to abolish slavery, among other achievements. His uncle and aunt, Thomas and Eleanor, were laid to rest in the local graveyard.

**Ecton Hall** is constructed of light coloured sandstone, carried across the valley from a demolished residence which had belonged to King John at Whiston. The Catesby family, whose kinsmen were involved in the Gunpowder Plot, owned the Elizabethan mansion.

**The church of St Mary Magdalene:** In July 1588, the tower (rebuilt in the 14th century at the time of the plague) of the church of St Mary Magdalene was chosen as the location for the beacon fire by the Lord Lieutenant of Northampton, to call the men to arms in the event of the Spanish invasion by the Armada.

The church has a number of memorials to prominent persons, including John Palmer, linguist and rector from 1641-1679, who built 'a school for poor children' and the rectory, now known as Ecton House, presently a Conference Centre and Retreat.

71

**The World's End** public house stands in place of a former coaching inn, the Globe, chronicled in 1678 when turnpikes were in operation. This consisted of a barrier being set across the road to ensure the collection of a toll before passing on. The pub was often visited by William Hogarth, the artist, who painted the first sign for the hostelry during the 18th century, reputedly to pay a debt!

After the Battle of Naseby in 1645 the victorious Roundheads tried to march their Royalist captives back to London. Many of the soldiers died of fatigue or fatal wounds as they passed this way, and it is thought the name was derived from that foray.

**Sywell Country Park:** There is a Countryside Ranger service, a Visitors Centre for leaflets and information, a Tree Trail around the magnificent specimens in the arboretum below the dam, picnic areas, day fishing, bird-watching, free car parking and toilets. Many events are staged in the park during the year, the ideal venue for everything from playschemes to sponsored runs.

The site was originally the water supply serving the districts of Rushden and Higham Ferrers, and some of the old pumps and machinery have been retained and restored for posterity. It was purchased in 1983 by Northants County Council and the 68 acres of water are surrounded by 143 acres of pasture and parkland.

Two of the disused filterbeds have been cleverly converted to provide an exciting pond-dipping waterbed, and over the fence, a specially designed butterfly garden, both with easy access for wheelchairs.

# Stoke Bruerne and Shutlanger: The Grand Union Canal

**Introduction:** Stoke Bruerne is on the Grand Union Canal, and a huge iron support from an old aqueduct adjacent to the car park for the Canal Museum is the first indication of the delights in store, both for the canal buff and the casual visitor. This fascinating walk follows the towpath toward the impressive Blisworth tunnel, then strikes up and across rolling wooded countryside to Shutlanger, with its medieval monastery.

Returning to the canal, a short detour follows the ascending flight of 7 locks, an opportunity to watch the river craft at close quarters as they make their way slowly up the 56 ft incline. The Canal Museum is well worth visiting with its large display of memorabilia, which began as the private collection of a former lock-keeper and illustrates the heyday of canal travel in the 18th and 19th centuries.

**Distance:** The complete circuit is just over 5 miles. Taking the shorter route, about 3 miles. OS Landranger 1:50,000 Sheet 152.

**Refreshments:** The Boat Inn quayside at Stoke Bruerne offers various facilities, and there are also cafes and shops waterside, some of which stay open in the winter. The Plough Inn is beside the path at Shutlanger.

**How to get there:** Stoke Bruerne is south of Northampton, not far from the M1 (junction 15), off the A508, and a similar distance from the A5. It is also within easy reach of Milton Keynes. There is a car park at the Canal Museum.

WALK ELEVEN

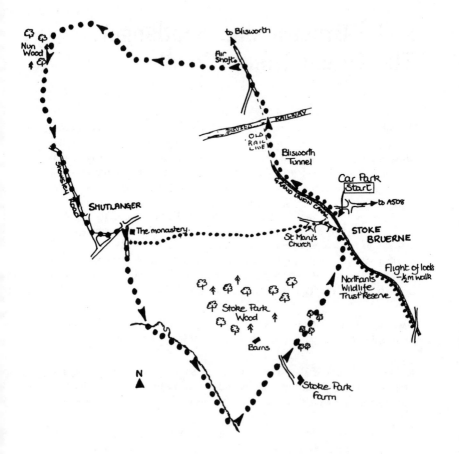

**The Walk:** Make your way to the quayside at the Canal Museum and then, staying on the nearside, walk to the right along the towpath, where hundreds of men and beasts have trod before, along the water's edge to the winding pool (used for turning boats). Just out of sight beyond the bend is the red brick face of the Blisworth Tunnel, dark, dank and dripping. Eerie sounds issue forth when an unseen boat is approaching! The brick hut beside it was to shelter men and animals.

Walk up the slope, where the horses used to be led, and straight ahead between the trees, which was the original course of the Blisworth Hill Railway. The rails were removed and used again as track on another section at Gayton.

Continue forward, past the remains of the conventional railway bridge, until the track converges with the road to Blisworth, then in about 50 yards, before Buttermilk Hall Farm, turn left into a series of fields. A ventilation shaft to the canal tunnel, one of many though some are now obscured by overgrowth, and a pond are to the right. Keep straight on, with a view of St Mary's church to the left, to a big oak tree with a waymark, staying close to the hedge. Bear right, to a further gap with a barkless tree stump, along the brow of the hill with a sight of Blisworth to the right, around the edge of the field, to Nuns Wood. Stay outside the woodland, with vistas of undulating countryside, to farm sheds, and exit through a gate with fingerpost, to Showsley Road.

Down now into the village of Shutlanger, past the Manor House, turning into Twitch Hill and a jetty by the stream, coming out near to the Plough Inn. Left here, past the school with a handless clock and a handsome beech tree inside the wall, crossing to Water Lane, where the Monastery is hidden among the profusion of trees. Down the track a little way, a short cut goes back to Stoke Bruerne, toward St Mary's church.

Traverse an old ridge and furrow field, where a lone maple tree bears a waymark, and over the wooden bridge, keeping to the bank over 3 fields, following the winding brook (which flows into the river Tove) with Stoke Park Wood on the rise and Alderton in the distance.

Turn to the left over the stile, meadow and stream to an old metal gate, and note the red brick barns of unusual design with arched and gabled ends. Keep straight on, past Stoke Park Farm, and cross the lane, with poultry sheds to the left, passing next between an avenue of poplars.

Through the gate to a green lane bounding the old brickworks and quarry, now a Northants Wildlife Trust Reserve, noted for its variety of insects and particularly dragonflies in a superb habitat. Waterway Cottage and the road bridge will now be in sight.

Go over the bridge, or under, to Welshpool Lock (dry), with a gauging mechanism, and up the steps. Cross the mighty paddles and gates canalside, bordered by attractive cottages and gardens, and you are back at the Canal Museum where you began.

**A short option:** Crossing the bridge from the museum, take the towpath to the left as far as the Lock Keeper's Cottage, about ½ mile distant. An easy, winding path unfolds, where often ducks come racing out of the water, hopeful of tidbits. The ascending flight of 7 locks, carrying boats through a height of 56 ft provide added interest, particularly in summer when the movement of boats is constant.

## Historical Notes

**Stoke Bruerne and the Grand Union Canal:** The long arm of the Grand Union Canal in Northamptonshire played a major role in the industrialisation of Great Britain, causing sweeping changes in the late 1700s. The building of the canal network provided employment for men in many of the scattered communities, when over 80 Acts of Parliament were passed permitting the construction of the waterways, cutting canals and extending existing river courses. The main street of Stoke Bruerne was diverted and re-routed to accommodate this new venture.

Regent's Canal Dock in London, to the south, and Lancashire and Humberside to the north, were at the extreme ends of the system, enabling cargoes of coal and cereals to be moved between established points, such as mills and quays for loading, some now converted to modern use as private homes. The barges, or narrow boats, were drawn by horses treading the towpaths, hauling heavy burdens, and these became a familiar sight to country dwellers. Narrowboat people lived in cramped conditions. The proud owners, to this day, keep alive the tradition of 'roses and castles' hand painted on their floating homes, used too to decorate many utensils.

**The Canal Museum** (admission fee and please note limited winter hours) is located in a restored mid 19th century canalside cornmill, originally powered by a steam engine, where the adjoining stable block previously housed the essential horses. There are displays of working models and archive film of traditional boats of yesteryear, and costumes.

On the quay there are numerous amenities, including the Boat Inn and small stores. Boat trips operate in summer months close by and also at this time, canal craft fairs, waterway artists' exhibitions and other allied events are always popular. Picnic tables and benches are set beneath lofty poplars, with toilets on a lower level. Moored alongside the quays, the narrowboats, with their colourful embellishments, may be here for a day, or perhaps overnight. From the banks, the mixed rooftops of the village dwellings and the little hedgebound green fields make a charming backdrop.

**The Blisworth Tunnel:** There were 3 tunnels constructed in this county, the others being at Crick and Braunston. Preliminary work began on the Blisworth Tunnel in 1793, but stopped and started at irregular intervals as problems arose. It is 3,056 yards long and ultimately cost £90,003 2s 4d, about £30 per yard! It was at one time the longest (but was just pipped by Dudley Tunnel). When horses reached this section, they were walked over the top. Men lying on special boards affixed to the decks (examples in the museum), who were registered 'leggers', walked the vessel through the dark tunnel, treading the walls, taking 2½ hours to make the trip.

Prior to this arrangement, 5 years before the tunnel was opened in 1805, a primitive horse-drawn railway was built to carry cargoes on open wagons between the completed parts of the canal. This was later dismantled and used by horses only to pass over to the next section of the towpath. One story goes that the contractor excavating the tunnel was somewhat illiterate and made his calculations utilising the local church tower as his yardstick — which in fact, is quite clever!

Upon the introduction of steam tugs around 1871, proper ventilation in the tunnel was deemed necessary, and consequently a series of air shafts were sunk for this purpose. One of these may be seen on the walk, near to Buttermilk Hall Farm.

Commercial use of canals ceased by 1950, when it became more viable to transport goods by road or rail. It remains the longest tunnel still in use on the waterways system, and was reopened in 1984 by British Waterways after extensive repair work.

**Shutlanger:** The Monastery at Shutlanger is thought to have been a hostel or retreat for journeying monks, and the oldest part of this unusual private residence is the 13th century porch, leading to a stone spiral staircase.

A pastry roll with meat at one end and fruit at the other, known as a 'Shutlanger clanger', was taken as sustenance to the fields by working men, and sounds very substantial too!

# Cosgrove and Passenham: Water All The Way!

**Introduction:** Cosgrove has no through road, which is somewhat unusual, and was bisected by the advent of the Grand Union Canal, constructed in the 1800s. It is now a popular leisure area, where the slow-moving narrow boats pass, or moor temporarily along the banks. Some are decorated with the traditional bright motifs of roses and castles, tubs of flowers and gleaming brasses.

A spectacular viaduct, the Iron Trunk, is to be found to the south-east of the village and affords splendid pastoral views in all directions. Not only does it convey the canal over the river Great Ouse, but the walker too, before the latter descends to enjoy the riverside path, by a novel method. Quiet observation may be rewarded by the sight of a heron on these low lying fields and banks (which are liable to flood in winter), or more rarely, the flash of a brilliant kingfisher darting over the stream.

An easy path winds through the Ouse Valley Park, a sanctuary for wildlife, to the bridge at Old Stratford and on to the old forest village of Passenham. The walker returns via pasture and arable fields, using the shady elevated towpath beside the disused bed of the former Stratford and Buckingham Arm of the canal. Views of the early 18th century Cosgrove Hall, parkland and church unfold, before passing over the lock-gates and under the canal again, through a horseshoe-shaped culvert, completing the circuit without even wetting the feet!

**Distance:** 5½ miles, or 3½ miles excluding the walk to Passenham. OS Landranger 1:50,000 Sheet 152.

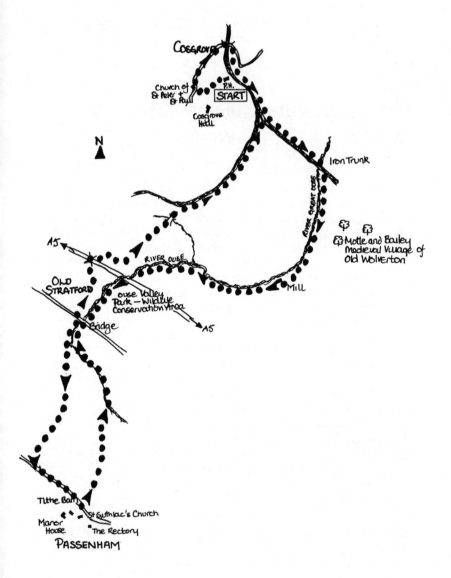

COSGROVE

Church of
St Peter +
St Paul

P.H.
START

Cosgrove
Hall

N

Iron Trunk

A5

RIVER OUSE

RIVER GREAT OUSE

Motte and Bailey
Medieval Village of
Old Wolverton

OLD
STRATFORD

Ouse Valley
Park — Wildlife
Conservation Area

Mill

Bridge

A5

Tithe Barn

St Guthlac's Church

Manor
House

The Rectory

PASSENHAM

**Refreshments:** At Cosgrove there is a shop, the Barley Mow public house and an hotel, The Old Bakery, just off the route, in the village. The Garden Shop canalside, offers refreshments in the summer months.

**How to get there:** Cosgrove is 12 miles from Northampton on the A508 to Watling Street (A5), turning off to the east for ¾ mile. The city of Milton Keynes is not far away. Park near the Barley Mow public house.

**The Walk:** From the Barley Mow, just off the main street at Cosgrove, walk down to the worn, but handsome, stone bridge over the Grand Union Canal.

Descend directly to the right, to the towpath, and be sure not to miss the captivating setting of the bridge. Carry on, above the 7 lagoons of the leisure park below. These were formed by old sand and gravel workings, exhausted by the demand in the construction of the M1. Remnants of the narrow-gauge rails remain embedded in the bank.

Keep to the main channel of the canal, past the junction of the defunct Old Stratford and Buckingham Arm, the lock and winding pool. This short stretch of the Grafton Way, which in turn links with the North Bucks Way, brings you to the aptly named Iron Trunk, or Pig Trough.

Good views, and a 3-fingered post here, before going down the steps to the horseshoe-shaped low tunnel, sometimes known as a 'cattle-creep', to the level of the river Great Ouse. Only vague traces linger of the early flight of locks, in use before the viaduct came into being. Across the fields beside the firm path, towards Wolverton, lies the site of the medieval village, terraces, motte and bailey, now almost swamped by trees.

You next come to a rather gaunt place, Wolverton Mill, which still houses much of the working gear. The race and weir are next, before following through the Ouse Valley Park. Go under the wide span of the A5, via conservation area and lakes, to the long bridge at Old Stratford.

Cross to the opposite pavement, and river, to a fingerpost and through a jetty between a crescent of houses, obviously built on the existing line of the footpath. Leave by a similar short alleyway, and forward over several fields to exit left in the quiet lane into Passenham, partially hidden by tall trees.

The church of St Guthlac, the rectory, manor house and tithe barns are all in close proximity and set together in the midst of this tiny hamlet, at present an oasis of tranquillity. Further along the single street, the renovated mill borders the river. The fingerpost directs the walker back across the water-meadows to the main bridge at Old Stratford.

Once there re-cross the road and go down the slope to return on the opposite side of the river, to a stile, and follow the waymark to a track and new bridge over the A5. On the other side walk along the edge of the field parallel to the road for a short way, then left down the bank to the brook and over the little bridge. Head for a line of trees and a distant white post.

The old towpath runs along an embankment above the disused arm of the Stratford Canal, which is colonised by copious reed-beds and hosts of grasses, wildflowers and brambles. This forms a handy habitat and natural 'corridor' for some of the more secretive animals, above the open fields. A panorama of patchwork fields and dense stands of trees, in subtle hues, make this an excellent viewpoint, while Cosgrove Hall, on the hill amid surrounding parkland, and the church of St Peter and St Paul form a picturesque tableau.

Stay beside the private moorings of the backwater and cross by the lock-gates, adjacent to the Garden Shop. Retrace your route along the towpath to steps down the bank and under another eerie tunnel beneath the canal, emerging in sight of the Barley Mow.

A loop around the lovely church is recommended, either at the beginning or end of the walk. From the pub, turn left into the main street and just past The Stocks follow the wall of Medlar House, which was the rectory, which leads to the black iron gates of St Peter and St Paul's. To the side of the church, the leaning stone wall in Church Walk, bordering the graveyard, gives way to open fields and the canal and ends with a kissing-gate, close to the pub.

## Historical Notes

**Cosgrove:** In 1793, George III approved an Act of Parliament which resulted in the Grand Union Canal Company constructing a canal from Braunston, through Buckinghamshire and Hertfordshire, to the river Thames at Brentford in Middlesex. The 2 halves of that waterway met at Cosgrove. The unique cast-iron Iron Trunk, 101 ft long, 15 ft wide and 36 ft above the river, is supported on sturdy pillars and was made at Ketley Iron Works. It was designed by William Jessop, the engineer who had been responsible for the canal, to replace the original stone aqueduct, which had previously collapsed in 1808.

As the Roman road Watling Street (A5), running between Dover and the fortress town of Chester, is only a mile away, it is hardly surprising that the site of a Roman bath-house complex was discovered in recent years just below Cosgrove Hall. One of the baths was found to be lead-lined, and there were traces of a system of flues, which channelled heat from a furnace as required.

**The church of St Peter and St Paul** is usually unlocked during the day, and the cobbled patch and an old iron foot-scraper invite the visitor to open the door and look inside.

The 14th century tower houses 6 bells, the oldest being from the 15th century, and a round copper-faced clock. St Peter's symbolises a typical village church, and all one could wish for in a rural community. It is beautifully tended and obviously much loved. The scarlet-lined doors and carpets glow against the more sombre interior. There is a fine oak-timbered roof, decorated organ pipes, stained glass windows, and embroidered hassocks between the pews.

**Old Stratford:** Mention is made of a stone bridge over the Ouse here in 1594, and it is thought that a wooden bridge was in existence prior to that date. There would also have been a tollgate at one time.

Launches and steam tugboats were built for export by Edward Hayes in his yard at Wharf Lane, from the early 19th century, until its closure in 1925. They were sent all over the world, to India, Russia, and even to the Nile!

**Passenham:** This parish, now enhanced and almost hidden by glorious trees, was once part of the vast Royal hunting forest of Whittlewood, comprising mainly oaks and covering about 32 square miles. At the far end of the village stands the 13th century mill, beside the river which winds through this alluvial plain.

**The church of St Guthlac:** The dedication is said to relate to a Mercian figure of the 8th century. He was a descendant of that royal house who chose to become a hermit and was later canonised. An early reference to the church of St Guthlac was made in the reign of Henry I (1100-1135), who gave it into the care of the newly founded Abbey of Cirencester, and it remained thus until the 16th century. Thought to be from the 13th century, the present building has had many additions. In the 14th century the tower was built, but the spire collapsed 3 centuries later, causing the tower itself to be reconstructed.

The chancel was rebuilt and elaborately decorated in the 2 years after 1626 by Sir Robert Banastre, lord of the manor. He was knighted in 1605 by James I, to whom he was Comptroller of the Household, and was Court Victualler to Charles I. Sir Robert's marble memorial on an interior wall displays his bust, with his epitaph on a black tablet below listing his attributes. He was, however, said to have been a hard man, who died a violent death at the age of 80 years as a result of a hunting accident. It follows that his ghost now returns, furiously driving a coach and horses through the village.

Important wall paintings of 4 Old Testament prophets, 4 Evangelists and other religious figures adorn the shell-arched niches divided by pilasters. These were brought to light and painstakingly restored in the 1950s. There is a Jacobean oak pulpit featuring the emblem of the Stuart arms, a gallery and box pews from the 18th century, and stained glass, all of great interest.

Sir Robert also constructed the smaller of the 2 tithe barns for the storage of crops, and is thought to have carried out the repair or rebuilding of the rectory, noted as the ancient seat of the family.

# Sulgrave, Weston & Lois Weedon: Manors & Memorials

**Introduction:** The ancestral home of George Washington and by contrast a piece by the modern sculptor Henry Moore, are unexpected finds within a 3 mile radius in the remote environs of the heart of England!

Many American visitors make this area their mecca in their search for their early connections, and no doubt pay homage to their presidential forefather in the simple 14th century church of St James the Less at Sulgrave. It would be sad to venture no further however, and miss the chance to stand on the old castle site or put a limb through the ancient stocks on the green, underneath the majestic beeches.

The linking neighbouring communities of Weston and Lois Weedon, both known under a variety of names over the years, share the essentials of country life. The pub is in the former, and the church in the latter, and the seat of learning somewhere in between! At Lois Weedon we find Henry Moore's moving memorial to Dame Edith Sitwell. Wide open spaces separate Sulgrave from these quiet places, in this pretty part of the south-west of the county.

**Distance:** The walk is about 6 miles, taking 3 hours, but more time might be allowed to take in the points of interest. OS Landranger 1:50,000 Sheet 152.

**Refreshments:** At Sulgrave there is the Star Inn and the Thatched House Hotel, almost opposite the manor. There is also a village shop. The Crown public house is at the T-junction in the centre of Weston.

**How to get there:** Sulgrave is just off the B4525 from Northampton to Banbury. Park in Sulgrave village — the walk begins from Manor Road, near the gates to Sulgrave Manor.

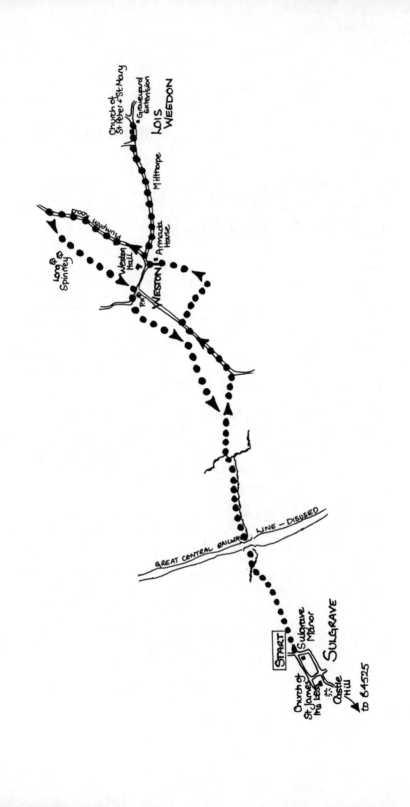

**The Walk:** Leave Sulgrave village by the bridleway at the far end of Manor Road, to the east of the gateway to the distinctive Sulgrave Manor. Walk the track at first between double hedges, to pass under the bridge of the disused Great Central Railway line, which has been closed for some years.

The path forward is easily followed alongside the brook and through to the 'Bridleway' post on the Helmdon to Weston Road. Turn to the left, towards Weston. No sign of human habitation so far, as the hill to the left sweeps up in a 'double hump', with wide verges.

Follow the road until, on the brow of the short, steep hill, a 'Footpath' sign indicates the way to the right, at right angles to the road, along the ridge, offering fine views of the undulating landscape.

Watch out for the stile in the hedgerow and go straight down the field, making for Weston again and a series of paddocks for horses. In the surrounding wooden rails just prior to the metal gate across the track, use the gate to go toward the hidden brook in the dip. Cross by the bridge and turn left beside a high stone wall, to emerge at the picturesque Armada House on the green, opposite the walled grounds of elegant Weston Hall.

Turn to the right, past the Plumpton Road and the spreading chestnut tree, up the hill. The hard path is set well back from the verge and has a wayside seat. Very soon, in ¾ mile, Lois Weedon comes into sight.

Be sure to carry on down the hill, over Milthorpe, to the lovely little church, with 'herringbone' traces in the ancient stonework on the west wall. Over the road, in the extension to the graveyard, is the last resting place of Dame Edith Sitwell, in a tranquil setting of utter peace and quiet.

Retrace your steps now and turn into Plumpton Road for a short distance, past a couple of dwellings, to a fingerpost and stile on the left. This part of the walk crosses old ridge and furrow sheep pastures, and at the tail end of Long Spinney, bear to the right over 2 more fields to re-enter Weston, between houses, almost opposite the Crown public house.

Turn right, by the old 18th century Baptist Chapel with its unusual pyramid roof and elongated windows with rows of square panes, to Grove Lane set back from the street on the same side.

Almost immediately, the stile and fingerpost are atop an abrupt bank on the left. Follow up and over 2 fields and then downhill, bearing slightly to the right, to rejoin the first bridleway. Return under the old rail line with the woody banks to Sulgrave, with the bonus of the rolling countryside stretching away to the horizon.

## Historical Notes

**Sulgrave Manor:** The manor here was first mentioned in the Domesday survey and later belonged to the Priory of St Andrew at Northampton, reverting to the Crown in 1539. Henry VIII sold it to Lawrence Washington, who was a prosperous wool-stapler and Mayor of Northampton, and a cousin of Lady Spencer at Althorp. He was responsible for further building and was the ancestor of George Washington. He raised a large family, by 2 wives, and their descendants continued to live in the manor for the next 120 years, until it went out of their line. On the gable of the new porch, he incorporated the coat of arms of Queen Elizabeth, and the manor is now one of the listed buildings within the parish.

Legend has it that Elizabeth, then a princess, was given refuge here when fleeing from the wrath of her sister, Queen Mary. She had been held in captivity at Woodstock and had escaped with her supporters, in the hope of reaching the continent. Sir Thomas Tresham, the Sheriff of the county, and his men were seeking to waylay the group but failed, and Elizabeth is said to have left her hiding place in the roof space at the manor and returned to Woodstock unharmed.

Colonel John Washington, in 1656, sailed for Virginia. He was the grandfather of George, the first President of the United States, and the house is now in the joint ownership of the Peoples of Great Britain and the United States of America. It was presented by British subscribers in 1914, to celebrate the Hundred Years of Peace between the 2 countries.

All the rooms at the manor are furnished in either the Tudor or Queen Anne style. The gardens, Brew House, Courtyard, Museum and Brass Rubbing Centre are open to the public on most days throughout the year, with the exception of January.

**The church of St James the Less**, built in the 14th century, has a tower base of Saxon origin. Enter by the splendid lychgate, with the old castle site, now merely a mound, just over the low wall surrounding the graveyard. Nothing more remains after excavations revealed traces of a large timbered hall from the 11th century and signs of a later stone edifice.

Over the south porch the date 1564 is inscribed, and just inside the door a huge chest stands solidly on the floor, bound with heavy iron trappings. The octagonal font, from the 15th century, is decorated with ornamental leaf design.

The Washington Pew is open, and set in a corner in the south aisle, at right angles to the seating for the congregation, with the family tomb in front. Above is a brass plate to Lawrence Washington, who died in 1584, and his wife. Four panels of Elizabethan glass are high in the wall.

**Weston:** The village is also recorded as Weston by Weedon. Formerly an Elizabethan manor, the mellowed Armada House sits resplendent, recessed from the road. It is gabled and dormered, with mullioned and transomed windows, and was constructed in the year of the anticipated invasion by the Spanish Armada, 1588.

**Lois Weedon:** In the 11th century, a castle is chronicled at Weedone or Weedon Pinkney. The place has also been known as St Loys, Loys Weedon and Weedon Lois. No trace lingers of the 11th century priory, except for the medieval fishponds at the foot of the slope in a field called Church Close, beyond the cemetery. The monks used a well, fed from the source of a mineral-enriched spring believed to have healing properties, which became known as St Loys' Well.

The cruciform church of St Peter and St Mary, on a hill among dark cypresses and cedars, was the scene of a dramatic incident in July 1643, during the Civil War. Parliamentary soldiers went to the church to arrest the Anglican priest, William Losse. He shrewdly barricaded himself in the tower and resisted the troop of emissaries, outwitting them with great courage and perspicacity, until they departed, minus their intended prisoner!

Members of the Sitwell family, 3 of whom were English poets, are buried in the extension to the graveyard. On the tall, tapering memorial slab to Dame Edith, who died in 1964, is mounted a bronze plaque in the form of 2 delicate hands, representing Youth and Age, by the celebrated sculptor, Henry Moore.

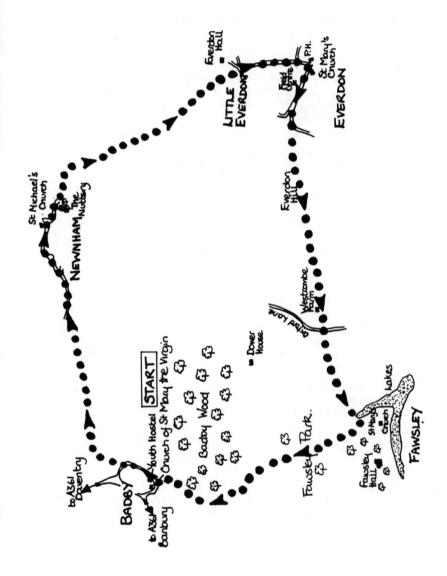

# Badby, Newnham, The Everdons and Fawsley

**Introduction:** The walker here, in close proximity to the Cotswolds, has the promise of a plethora of stunning landscapes. Ancient ridge and furrow meadows on gentle slopes dotted about with woodland, laced with charming villages, combine to make this a rewarding 'up hill and down dale' trail.

The first part of the walk, from Badby to the pretty hamlet of Little Everdon, follows the Nene Way and consequently is well posted. The plateau of Everdon Hill affords marvellous views, and the route then leads towards Fawsley, with its picturesque ruined Dower House (and ghost!) and landscape created by Capability Brown. The views from here are a temptation to pause awhile, before joining another county path, the Knightley Way, through rolling pastureland. If it is bluebell time when you walk here, the woodland path will be a special delight.

**Distance:** About 6 miles — time unlimited, as you may wish to stop for a 'breather' or for pure pleasure. OS Landranger 1:50,000 Sheet 152.

**Refreshments:** In Badby, the Maltsters Arms and the Windmill offer refreshments. Newnham has the Romer Arms facing the green. The Plough Inn at Great Everdon is adjacent to the church and all 3 villages have small shops.

**How to get there:** Badby is on the A361 Daventry to Banbury road and is located 4 miles due west of Weedon on the A45 from Northampton. There are regular weekday bus services on the Daventry route only.

**The Walk:** Start in Badby at Church Green, opposite the Youth Hostel, formerly a 17th century cottage, then take Brookside Lane, bearing left into Chapel Lane. On the edge of the village follow the Nene Way oak post directing alongside the stream, over the stile and little bridge, and around the perimeter of low lying fields, beneath the willows, to Newnham.

The circular wrought iron seat encircling the tree on the green at Newnham is handy for a rest, near to the Romer Arms. Walk up School Hill past the triangle with the thatched barn and well, standing back from the War Memorial, as far as St Michael's church with its unusual porch. The cobbled path meanders through the graveyard, graced by worn headstones and an intriguing ornate vault with arches and inscriptions. The shady cutting between stone walls bedecked with mosses and trailing ivy emerges at a quaint well with a slate roof and an iron handle. Follow the signs down the leafy lane and left, past The Nuttery, set amidst hazel nut orchards.

Through the gate look for a trio of willows and a lone telegraph pole with a waymark and continue on the Nene Way. Strike off across the old ridge and furrow meadows to a solid wooden bridge, and perhaps the occasional arable field, in a slightly diagonal direction. The white gates bordering the private parkland mark the boundary of Everdon Hall, complete with a traditional English thatched cricket pavilion in the grounds. Skirting the Hall, the path leads to steps fashioned in a pretty stone wall topped by railings, at the hub of this picturesque hamlet.

Leaving the Nene Way, walk up the hill to neighbouring Great Everdon, facing St Mary's church and the Plough Inn. Further on, note the Everdon Field Centre, a popular venue for children and those seeking further historical and botanical information. Bear left at the road fork going out of the village. On the bend of the short steep incline, look for steps, stile and fingerpost 'to Fawsley'. This leads over Everdon Hill (1 mile), opening to a panorama of undulating countryside, finally descending to the left of Westcombe Farm.

Cross Oxford Lane (Newnham to Preston Capes road) past farmyard and pens, and straight up again, then down the slope of Temple Hill, catching a brief glimpse of the sadly derelict Dower House in Fawsley Park.

Bear to the left toward the distant isolated church of St Mary and the serene lakes created long ago by Capability Brown, and the splendid facade of Fawsley Hall, seen through the cloak of trees. Given this enchanting spread, the walker might care to dally here awhile and enjoy the delights of these most pleasant environs.

The circular white discs marking another County Path, the Knightley Way, will now be in evidence, and are set back from the curve of the lane. Follow these across the fields to the up-and-over ladder stile and rolling parkland studded with stately beeches, to Badby Woods.

The trodden path stays just inside the woodland, and in springtime draws many a visitor to admire the carpet of bluebells in a riot of soft colour. Over 2 fields, nestled among the trees, Badby village peeps from the dells ahead.

## Historical Notes

**Badby:** Badby lies on a low rounded hill of clay, embracing some minor earthworks in the vicinity which through the years have yielded a quantity of flints and pottery. Mentioned as early as AD 833, the manor of Badby was granted to the Abbey of Croyland by the King of Mercia, and later, after a series of changes, passed to the Abbey of Evesham. The early courthouse was surrounded by a moat, and attended by the Abbot, who would visit to collect the dues. At the time of the Domesday survey it was returned to Croyland Abbey. In 1246, Badby Wood was enclosed as parkland by permission of the Crown, at the instigation of the Abbot.

After the Dissolution of the Monasteries, King Henry VIII granted an exchange of the lordships of Badby and Newnham, for the manor of Blisworth, to Sir Edmund Knightley. Thus the properties remained in the care of his descendants for the next 500 years, gaining wealth from sheep farming.

There are several interesting old cottages, not least among them the charity school for girls, founded by the Knightleys (now Village Hall Cottages). These pupils included a few boarders and the young ones were often taken over to Fawsley Hill to be instructed in domestic skills.

Stone pits around the village produced quantities of materials used in the local dwellings, along with clay, sand and gravel for the brick kilns. Wheelwrights and carpenters made wheels and hurdles, and the blacksmiths played their part in the community. Tailoring and bootmaking took place and a large number of the inhabitants were employed on the neighbouring estate.

For several generations members of the Spencer family, now related to our Royal Family, were in residence here before moving to Everdon, and latterly to Althorp.

**The church of St Mary the Virgin**, seen at the beginning of the walk, dates back to the 14th century, but as with any ancient places of worship, had additions of Gothic and Georgian styles, and a later Victorian window in the tower. The 6 bells bear various inscriptions, and have strict usage for individual occasions such as weddings, funerals and divine services.

**Everdon:** Poet Thomas Gray (1716-1771) often stayed with his uncle, Rev Antrobus, at the rectory. Many believe that this churchyard is featured in his famous *Elegy*, rather than the generally accepted one at Stoke Poges. Both men were scholars, the elder his tutor at Eton College, and the younger, student and poet.

**Fawsley Manor:** Listed in an Anglo Saxon charter in the 10th century, together with Badby, Newnham and Everdon, all were part of a large estate, the boundary being the old Roman road, Watling Street. In the reign of Henry III in 1224, the owner was listed as Hugh Russell, who was granted the right to hold a market every Sunday. His heirs, the de Capes, next held the manor, until eventually it was sold to Simon de Fawsley.

The Knightleys evicted the local peasants in the latter half of the 15th century and enclosed the land so that they could graze sheep, which provided the family with wealth. The Knightley family, who hailed from Staffordshire, were resident here for hundreds of years. Charles I hunted in the surrounding deer park before the Battle of Naseby, when his troops were encamped at Borough Hill, close to Daventry.

The medieval church is dedicated to St Mary. Encircled by a ha ha (ditch), it is still used for worship throughout the year. The splendid alabaster tomb of 1534, depicts Sir Richard Knightley (nephew of Sir Edmund) and his wife, with their daughters and 8 sons. There are also intricately carved pews and treasured medieval stained glass.

The handsome facade of Fawsley Hall, with its elegant windows, stands resplendent among the quiet green pastures, veiled by majestic trees. The medieval Great Hall was possibly commissioned in 1530 by Sir Edmund Knightley, who died in 1542, with stout walls, a huge timbered roof and painted shields displayed. The ornate oriel windows from the 16th century face the church, and the inner courtyard is enclosed by Tudor walls. Other wings have been added in succeeding years. It is said that Queen Elizabeth I conferred a knighthood on the sons of Sir Richard when holding court in the Hall.

Servicemen stationed here during the Second World War caused much internal damage, scarring this noble edifice, and it was even put to use as a timber factory in the intervening years. However, it seems that nothing can totally destroy the Hall, for it is now being sensitively restored to its former glory by a dedicated private owner.

**The Dower House**, thought to be the earliest brick house in the county, was built for Lady Ursula Knightley, wife of Sir Edmund, in the 16th century. As was the custom of their time, widowed dowagers moved into their own residences when their successors took over the estates.

Carpenters working on the house made carvings featuring the old nursery rhyme 'Hey Diddle Diddle', which have since been placed in the church for safe keeping. The story illustrated on the panels has been suggested as a direct criticism of Richard III's seizure of the throne.

A later Lady Knightley allowed the tragic Elephant Man, a strange cloaked figure, to roam about in Badby Woods, which were then closed to the public. She had heard of his plight, incarcerated in the London Hospital, and of his longing to see the countryside, through the surgeon of that establishment. It was the same Lady Knightley who planted an avenue of cherry trees in these woods to enable her feathered friends to gather the fruits.

The house is now merely a sad reflection of its former self, overgrown and neglected, with the twisted chimneys lying in undignified disarray. A tragic ending to a fine building, deserted since the 18th century.

The ghost of a hunter is purported to appear round about the isolated Dower House, blowing his horn as he gallops through the night!

# Acknowledgements

Jane Draper for maps

Marian Pipe for moral support!

Dorothy Amos

Carl Hector

Colin Eaton and friends at Countryside Services N.C.C., for their unstinted assistance in various fields, and the co-operation of all the Footpath Officers.

Also for those stalwart souls who sometimes kept me company en route.